EXERCISE IN ACTION
CORE

EXERCISE IN ACTION
CORE

Hollis Lance Liebman

THUNDER BAY
P·R·E·S·S
San Diego, California

Thunder Bay Press
An imprint of the Baker & Taylor Publishing Group
10350 Barnes Canyon Road, San Diego, CA 92121
www.thunderbaybooks.com

Library of Congress Cataloging-in-Publication Data

Liebman, Hollis Lance.
  Exercise in action: core / Hollis Lance Liebman.
    pages cm.
  ISBN 978-1-62686-052-0 (pbk.) -- ISBN 1-62686-052-1 ()
1. Physical fitness. 2. Exercise. 3. Muscle strength. I. Title.
  GV841.L54 2014
  613.7'1--dc23
                                    2013043438

Printed in China
1 2 3 4 5 18 17 16 15 14

INTRODUCTION   6

STRETCHES AND WARM-UPS   8
  Supine Low Back Stretch   10
  Seated Spinal Stretch   11
  Adductor Stretch   12
  Cobra Stretch   13
  Iliotibial Band Stretch   14
  Hip to Thigh Stretch   15
  Lumbar Stretch   16
  Priformis Stretch   17
  Side Bends   18
  Swiss Ball Abdominal Stretch   19

SWISS BALL EXERCISES   20
  Swiss Ball Jackknife   22
  Swiss Ball Crunch   23
  Swiss Ball Forward Roll   24
  Swiss Ball Pike   26
  Swiss Plank with Leg Lift   27
  Swiss Ball Walk-Around   28
  Lying Leg Rotation   30
  Swiss Ball Push-Up   32
  Hip Crossover   33

MEDICINE BALL EXERCISES   34
  Medicine Ball Throw   36
  Big Circles with Medicine Ball   38
  Medicine Ball Pullover
    on a Swiss Ball   40
  Medicine Ball Push-Up   42
  Walk-Over   43
  Sit-Up and Throw   44
  Medicine Ball Slam   46
  Power Squat   47

CONTENTS

BODY WEIGHT EXERCISES 48

Step-Down 50

Tendon Stretch 51

McGill Curl-Up 52

Abdominal Kick-Out 53

Sit-Up 54

Alternating Sit-Up 55

Crunch 56

Alternating Crunch 57

Side Raised-Legs Crunch 58

Double-Leg Ab Press 59

Lemon Squeezer 60

Chair Abdominal Crunch 61

Oblique Roll-Down 62

Quadruped Lateral Lift 63

Abdominal Hip Lift 64

Hand Walkout 65

Kneeling Side Kick 66

Thigh Rock-Back 68

Standing Knee Crunch 69

Bridge 70

Bridge with Leg Lift 71

V-Up 72

Scissors 73

Leg Raises 74

Single-Leg Circles 75

Front Plank 76

Plank-Ups 77

Plank Roll-Down 78

Knee-Pull Plank 80

Reverse Plank 81

Side-Bend Plank 82

Tiny Steps 83

Advanced Superman 84

Prone Heel Beats 85

Mountain Climber 86

Push-Up 87

Chair Pose 88

Side-Lift Bend 89

Quadruped 90

Clamshell Series 92

Hand-to-Toe Lift 94

Kneeling Side Lift 95

Lateral Low Lunge 96

High Lunge 97

Towel Fly 98

Body Saw 99

Swimming 100

Hip Twist 101

Russian Twist 102

Twist 103

FREE WEIGHT EXERCISES 104

Kettlebell Figure-Eight 106

Turkish Get-Up 108

Wheel Rollout 110

Dumbbell Sit-Up 111

Kettlebell Double Clean 112

Stiff-Leg Dead Lift 113

Seated Barbell Twist 114

Standing Plate Twist 115

Seated Dumbell Press 116

Kettlebell Squat 117

CABLE AND BAND EXERCISES 118

Standing Cable Lift 120

Kneeling Cable Crunch 122

Standing Cable Crunch 123

Cable Rotations 124

Triceps Overhead Extension
   with Bands 125

BOSU BALL EXERCISES 126

Bosu Ball Crunch 128

Bosu Ball Sit-Up 129

Bosu Ball Bicycle Crunches 130

Bosu Ball Leg Scissors 131

Bosu Ball Side Plank 132

Bosu Ball Seated Leg Tucks 133

FOAM ROLLER EXERCISES 134

Quadruped Knee Pull-In 136

Hamstring Roll 137

Single-Leg Calf Press 138

Roller Triceps Dip 139

Diagonal Crunch 140

Roller Push-Up 141

Supine Marches 142

Iliotibial Band Release 143

Bridge with Leg Lift 144

Bridge with Leg Lift II 146

Hamstring Pull-In 147

Straight-Leg Bicycle 148

Dead Bug 149

WORKOUTS 150

Beginner Workout 151

Rotational Workout 152

Erector Workout 154

Athlete Workout 156

Melting Pot Workout 157

Kamikaze Workout 158

ACKNOWLEDGMENTS 160

Introduction

Whether in movies, print, or sporting events, many forms of media have advertised, flaunted, and celebrated flat or visible abdominals and a strong core as desired perfection for decades (think of the Charles Atlas ads from the 1950s and beyond: "Do Bullies Kick Sand in Your Face?").

But athletes the world over train their core muscles not for appearance, but for performance. Motion, power, stability, and performance are all derived, driven, and dictated from the core first. Before tasks can be carried out through the other muscles of the body, the core is the nucleus through which all movement originates.

What exactly is the core? The core refers to all of the muscles in the lower trunk area, including the lower back, abdominals, and hips. These muscles work in conjunction to provide support and mobility, and it is through the combination of these muscles that all bodily movement—in every possible direction—originates.

Most visible of the core muscle group is the rectus abdominis, or "six-pack" as it's commonly known. The abs, which are but a part of the entire core, are responsible for spinal stability as well as shortening the distance between your torso and your hips. The muscles on either side of your abdominals are both the internal and external obliques, responsible for bending from side to side and torso rotation. The erector spinae, a Christmas tree-shaped muscle, is located at the lower back and is responsible for spinal stabilization as well as spinal movement. Lastly, the hips play a major role in core strength, with the hip flexors acting as the basement of this muscular complex, supporting movement and allowing you to flex your hips.

A strong core is of paramount importance in keeping one functionally sound and operational, it is also seen as visually attractive, as exhibited in the myriad bare midriffs adorning the dozens of magazine covers seen the world over.

The annual number of willing customers purchasing diet books, nutritional supplements, gym memberships, exercise equipment, and even surgeries amounts to big business: in 2011 in the U.S. alone, health-club membership totalled 51.4 million, and health-club industry revenue reached $21.4 billion.

We are bombarded daily through local gyms, produce markets, clothing stores, all forms of media, and even apps on our smartphones touting a strong and visible core as being king, but why exactly is core training so important? Aside from the obvious aesthetic benefits of maintaining a lean and tight core, the real-world benefits include an ease in performing everyday movements even as you age. Imagine waking up with a back devoid of pain, a less restrictive and impinging way of picking up and transporting a cumbersome box in your home or office, or even standing naturally straighter and taller without having to focus on doing so.

Core training is not just a lesson in preparedness, but rather an insurance policy for your health, keeping your human machine functional. Core training actually pays dividends for those directly connected—literally. Witness a pregnant mother-to-be. Pre- and postnatal core training during and following pregnancy will not only result in an easier and healthier delivery for the baby, but a speedy recovery process for the mother after delivery.

Maintaining a strong core will lend optimal support to ancillary (assisting) muscles. In fact, the core is so central to your body's total movement that it is called upon when firing each and every muscle: when in the midst of a squat, your core is engaged in order to maintain the integrity of vertical movement; when pressing dumbbells overhead, the core is firing and enabled in order to keep the body upright. Have you ever worked your triceps and discovered later that your midsection was quite sore? That's your core at work.

Furthermore, the usage of artificial supports, such as chair backs, has, for years, done a lot of the work that we would otherwise rely on our core muscles for—this, combined with lack of exercise and a poor modern diet, has led to a generation with undertrained cores, which in turn leads to poor posture, back problems, and obesity.

The core is further unique in that it is perhaps the one muscular system of the body that is trained for its compactness rather than the sheer volume of, for example, the chest or biceps, all the while assisting all of the other muscle groups in their functions.

Careful diligence is required to get the most out of your core—not only to prevent future physical impairment, but to achieve the best proper maintenance (and showcasing) of your core muscles.

All of the exercises described in this book are of the dynamic, or movement-through-action variety, rather than isometric or static exercises, which involve holding a given muscle in the contracted position for a given period of time. For those of you with sedentary vocations or lifestyles, this is the perfect book. You would be well advised to exercise your core regularly, and can develop an appropriate routine through these pages—the rewards you reap will be great.

Stretches and Warm-Ups

Warming up and stretching are as important to the human body as turning a key into a car's ignition before hitting 65 mph on the open highway. Cold and restricted muscles are less pliable and more susceptible to injury than warm and loose tissue is. They key is to not overdo it and to take a muscle only to its positive threshold in terms of movement and mobility.

Supine Low Back Stretch

The Supine Low Back Stretch is perfect for stretching the lower back and the glute muscles; it is suitable for all sports and activities.

Step 1 Begin by kneeling with your back straight and your arms by your sides.

Step 2 Slowly lean forward, placing your hands on the floor in front of you.

Step 3 Lower your head and arch your back until you feel a stretch in your lower back. Hold for 30 seconds, relax, and repeat for an additional 30 seconds.

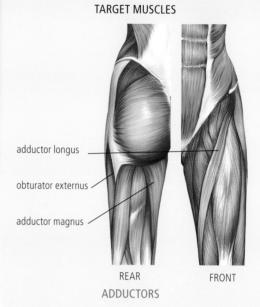

TARGET MUSCLES

adductor longus

obturator externus

adductor magnus

REAR   FRONT

ADDUCTORS

CORRECT ACTION
• Be sure to focus on a smooth, slow motion

AVOID
• Avoid arching your back too much

Seated Spinal Stretch

The Seated Spinal Stretch helps free up the spine and relieve the often constricted erector muscles.

WARNING Anyone with an atrophied lower back should avoid this routine.

Step 1 Sit on the floor with one leg stretched out in front of you.

Step 2 Cross your other leg over the outstretched leg, making sure the foot is flat on the ground. Keep one hand on the ground for support and the other placed over your bent leg.

Step 3 Rotate your torso away from the bent leg until your chest is nearly facing the opposite direction from the bent leg.

Step 4 Hold for 30 seconds, repeat, and then switch sides.

TARGET MUSCLES

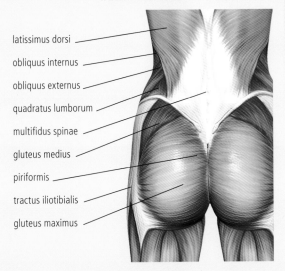

- latissimus dorsi
- obliquus internus
- obliquus externus
- quadratus lumborum
- multifidus spinae
- gluteus medius
- piriformis
- tractus iliotibialis
- gluteus maximus

SPINE AND ERECTOR

CORRECT ACTION
- Be sure to keep your back flat at all times

AVOID
- Don't excessively rotate your torso during the stretch

Adductor Stretch

This simple stretch, which works the adductors, takes about a minute to be most effective. As a general rule, the stretch should not hurt—there should be a gentle pulling sensation in the muscle.

Step 1 Stand tall with your feet wide apart.

Step 2 Bend your right leg while lowering your torso to the ground. Rest your hands on your thighs while you feel the deep stretch inside the left thigh.

Step 3 Hold for 30 seconds, relax, and repeat for another 30 seconds, then switch legs and repeat the exercise.

CORRECT ACTION
• Keep your torso upright

AVOID
• Overstretching your extended leg

TARGET MUSCLES

obturator
externus

adductor longus

adductor
magnus

ADDUCTORS

Cobra Stretch

This stretch helps loosen the spinal joints, and stretches your stomach, upper torso muscles, and the spine. It should only be used if you do not have previous back problems, because if done improperly it can cause vertebrae damage.

Step 1 Lie facedown with your arms bent, your elbows in, and your palms on the ground.

Step 2 Lift your upper body until your arms are at full length, bending your torso backward. Complete three repetitions of 15 seconds each.

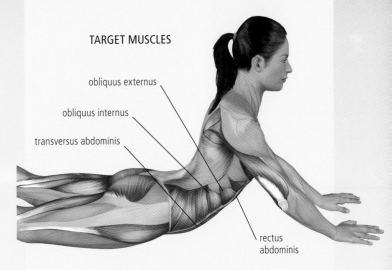

TARGET MUSCLES

obliquus externus

obliquus internus

transversus abdominis

rectus abdominis

OBLIQUES AND ABDOMINALS

CORRECT ACTION
• Keep your arms close to your sides

AVOID
• An excessive upward swing

Iliotibial Band Stretch

Stretching the IT band is rather different from stretching other muscles, as the IT band is a thick, fibrous fascia without the elasticity of your muscles. Iliotibial band stretches can make a big difference to back, hip, and knee problems.

TARGET MUSCLES

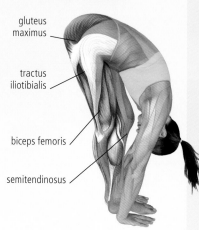

gluteus maximus

tractus iliotibialis

biceps femoris

semitendinosus

GLUTES AND TRACTUS ILIOTIBIALIS

Step 1 Start in a standing position, and cross your left foot behind the right ankle.

Step 2 Lean forward until you are as close to the floor with your fingertips as you can go. If you are able, grasp your toes, or, as a more difficult modification, place your hands flat on the floor.

Step 3 Hold for 20 seconds and repeat, then switch legs and repeat the entire stretch.

CORRECT ACTION
• Be sure to ease into the movement slowly

AVOID
• Overextending your legs

Hip to Thigh Stretch

Your hip flexors—which enable you to lift your knees and to bend at the waist—are located on your upper thighs, just below your hip bones. This exercise primarily targets both the hip flexors and the adductor muscles.

Step 1 Kneeling on your left knee, place your right foot on the floor in front of you so that your right knee is bent less than 90 degrees.

Step 2 Bring your torso forward, bending your right knee so that your knee shifts toward your toes. Keeping your torso in neutral position, press your right hip forward and downward to create a stretch over the front of your thigh. Raise your arms up toward the ceiling, keeping your shoulders relaxed.

Step 3 Bring your arms down and move your hips backward. Straighten your right leg, and bring your torso forward. Place your hands on either side of your straight leg for support.

Step 4 Hold for ten seconds, and repeat the forward and backward movement five times on each leg.

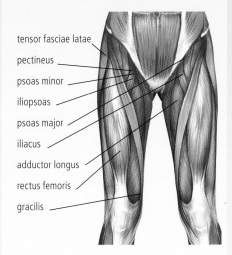

TARGET MUSCLES

tensor fasciae latae
pectineus
psoas minor
iliopsoas
psoas major
iliacus
adductor longus
rectus femoris
gracilis

HIP FLEXORS AND ADDUCTORS

CORRECT ACTION
- Your shoulders and neck should be relaxed
- Your entire body moves as one unit as you go into the stretch

AVOID
- Extending your front knee too far over the planted foot
- Rotating your hips
- Shifting the knee of the back leg outward

Lumbar Stretch

Everyday activities can result in tight back muscles, which over time can cause back pain and increase your risk of back injury. The Lumbar Stretch helps keep your spine flexible. It takes about two minutes to complete. This stretch is not advised if you have lower-back issues.

Step 1 Lie on your back with your legs bent to a 90-degree angle and your arms extended outward.

Step 2 Gently pull your knees over to your left side until the bottom knee almost touches the floor.

Step 3 Hold for 30 seconds, repeat, and then switch sides.

CORRECT ACTION
• Keep your back pressed flat against the floor

AVOID
• Jerking your leg hard across your side

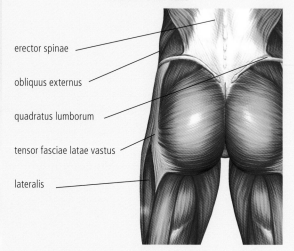

TARGET MUSCLES

erector spinae

obliquus externus

quadratus lumborum

tensor fasciae latae vastus

lateralis

LOWER BACK

MODIFICATION

1

2

Priformis Stretch

This move targets the gluteal and hip regions, and takes around two minutes to complete. The piriformis muscle laterally rotates and stabilizes the hip, and is important for athletes who participate in sports that require sudden changes of direction.

Step 1 Lie on your back with your left leg bent and your right ankle crossed over your left knee.

Step 2 Use your hands to grab the back of the left thigh close to the knee, and gently pull it toward your right shoulder.

Step 3 Hold for 30 seconds, relax, and repeat for another 30 seconds, then switch sides.

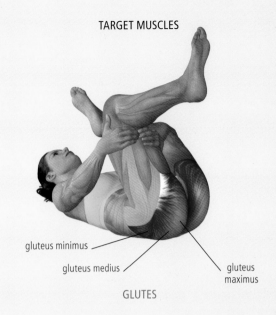

TARGET MUSCLES

gluteus minimus

gluteus medius

gluteus maximus

GLUTES

CORRECT ACTION
- Keep your back pressed to the ground

AVOID
- Excessively pulling on or straining the knee

Side Bends

Side Bends are perfect for stretching the serratus, oblique, and intercostal muscles. You should spend approximately one minute on this stretch. The exercise can be modified by placing one hand on your hip and one arm overhead (simpler) or by holding a weight or dumbbell overhead (more difficult).

Step 1 Begin by standing with your arms raised above your head and your fingers interlocked.

Step 2 Bend slowly to one side, keeping your fingers interlocked, then return to the vertical position.

Step 3 Repeat 10 times each side.

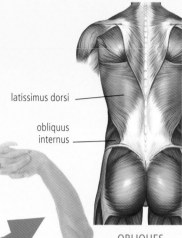

TARGET MUSCLES

latissimus dorsi

obliquus internus

OBLIQUES

MODIFICATION

CORRECT ACTION
• Be sure to keep your back straight

AVOID
• Bending forward or backward at the trunk

TARGET MUSCLES

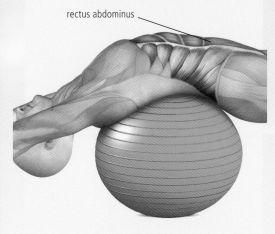

rectus abdominus

OBLIQUES AND ABDOMINALS

Swiss Ball Abdominal Stretch

The Swiss Ball Abdominal Stretch is a great supplement to your warm-up exercises. This focuses on warming and stretching the rectus abdominus muscles, but should be performed with great care.

Step 1 Begin by lying on your back on a Swiss ball with your feet shoulder-width apart and your arms stretched out straight behind your head.

Step 2 Reach your arms all the way backward until your hands touch the floor.

Step 3 While keeping your lower back on the ball, lower your hips and stretch your abdominals toward the ceiling.

Step 4 Hold for 30 seconds, relax, and repeat for an additional 30 seconds.

CORRECT ACTION
• Be sure to keep your torso planted on the ball

AVOID
• Try not to overextend your pelvic raise

Swiss Ball Exercises

The Swiss ball is a highly effective exercise tool for improving your body's balance and core strength while getting lean and toned. The instability of the ball is what the body responds to in order to remain balanced. It is filled with air and is available in various diameters—most commonly between 35 and 85 centimeters. It can be combined with weighted resistance or used effectively by itself for any body part, with a nearly unlimited range of angles and exercises.

Swiss Ball Jackknife

The Swiss Ball Jackknife is a strength builder—primarily in the trunk and hips. For proper performance, you need to use coordination, timing, accuracy, and strength.

Step 1 Assume a push-up position with your arms shoulder-width apart and your shins resting on the Swiss ball.

Step 2 Bend your knees, rolling the ball in toward your chest, keeping your arms straight the whole time.

Step 3 Extend your legs and repeat for 20 repetitions.

TARGET MUSCLES

obliquus externus

gluteus maximus

erector spinae

hip flexors

rectus abdominis

vastus lateralis

biceps femoris

TRUNK AND HIPS

CORRECT ACTION
• Keep a tight core throughout
• Proper breathing
• Keep your shoulders above your hands

AVOID
• A haphazard pattern
• Rounding your back
• Excessive speed

Swiss Ball Crunch

The Swiss Ball Crunch is a highly effective core strengthening exercise. A small step forward or backward can greatly decrease or increase the tension on the abdominal muscles.

Step 1 Begin by lying on your back on a Swiss ball with your head and neck supported, legs bent, your palms placed on your ears, and your elbows flared outward.

Step 2 Raise your head and shoulders off the ball while contracting your trunk toward your waist. Keep your lower back grounded on the ball.

Step 3 Lower your torso and repeat for 25 repetitions.

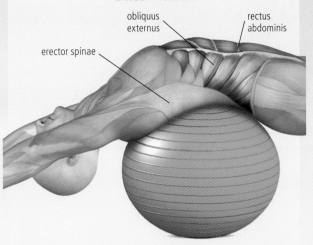

TARGET MUSCLES

obliquus externus

rectus abdominis

erector spinae

ABDOMINALS

CORRECT ACTION
- Maintain a precise and short range of motion
- Tension on the abdominals
- Contract the muscles at the top of your abdominals

AVOID
- Using the neck
- Bouncy and speedy repetitions
- Raising your lower back off the ball

Swiss Ball Forward Roll

The Swiss Ball Forward Roll is a key stabilizing exercise from which many movements can build. When holding this position, many of the key core muscles are activated. Recent studies have shown that the Swiss Ball Forward Roll activated more muscles in the rectus abdominis (the "six-pack muscle") and obliques than sit-ups and crunches.

Step 1 Kneel on the floor with your wrists resting on a Swiss ball with your upper back straight and firmly supported, your feet shoulder-width apart, your hips raised, and your arms outstretched to your sides.

Step 2 Roll the ball forward slowly, until your elbows are over the center of the ball.

Step 3 Hold this position for five seconds, then slowly reverse the movement and repeat ten times.

CORRECT ACTION
- Keep a tight core throughout the movement

AVOID
- A haphazard pattern
- Dropping your hips

1

TARGET MUSCLES

erector
spinae

obliquus
externus

gluteus
maximus

biceps
femoris

tibialis
anterior

hip flexors

rectus
abdominis

TRUNK AND LEGS

2

Swiss Ball Pike

The Swiss Ball Pike is a challenging core-strengthening exercise that requires balance, stability, and precision in order to complete with accuracy. It is a particularly effective abdominal-strengthening exercise.

Step 1 Begin in a standard push-up position with your body straight, your core contracted, and shins resting on a Swiss ball.

Step 2 Start by raising your hips toward the ceiling like a drawbridge, while keeping your core in check, rolling the Swiss ball in.

Step 3 Hold for 5 seconds; lower and repeat 5 times.

TARGET MUSCLES

gluteus maximus
biceps femoris
tibialis anterior
hip flexors
erector spinae
rectus abdominis

ABDOMINALS AND HIPS

1

2

CORRECT ACTION
- A controlled range of motion
- Be sure to lift using primarily your lower-back muscles

AVOID
- Excessive speed
- Dipping below parallel to the ground
- Using too much neck

Swiss Plank with Leg Lift

This exercise increases your ability to support your own body weight. It is a great exercise for the abdominals, and helps build upper-body strength. It can be made easier by just performing a plank (not raising your feet off the Swiss ball).

Step 1 Position yourself on all fours, with a Swiss ball by your feet. Plant your hands on the ground with your arms fully extended, and place your left foot on top of the Swiss ball.

Step 2 Carefully place your right foot on top of the Swiss ball too, and extend your legs fully.

Step 3 Raise your right foot off the ball and remain suspended in the plank position for 30 seconds (building up to 60 seconds). Replace your right foot and repeat with the left.

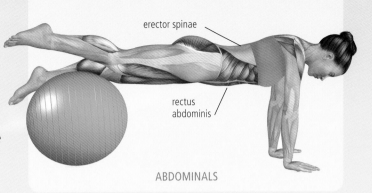

TARGET MUSCLES

erector spinae

rectus abdominis

ABDOMINALS

CORRECT ACTION
- Keep your abdominal muscles tight and your body in a straight line

AVOID
- Bridging too high, since this can take stress off the working muscles

Swiss Ball Walk-Around

The Swiss Ball Walk-Around is a challenging core-stabilizing exercise that requires balance and precision to complete with accuracy. It will pay great dividends if you make it a regular part of your workout. This is also a great exercise for shoulder stabilization—the purpose is to load each shoulder independently while maintaining a strong core and contracting the postural muscles.

CORRECT ACTION

- Keep your body elevated parallel to the ground or higher
- Be sure to keep the Swiss ball still and centered

AVOID

- Excessive speed
- Dipping below parallel to the ground
- Excessive strain on the wrists

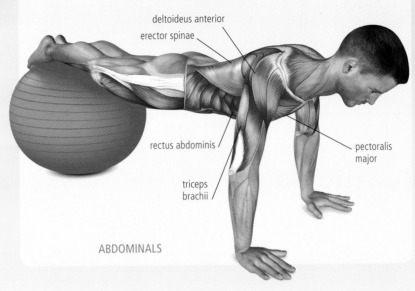

TARGET MUSCLES

deltoideus anterior

erector spinae

rectus abdominis

triceps brachii

pectoralis major

ABDOMINALS

Step 1 Begin in a push-up position with your shins on a Swiss ball.

Step 2 Walk sideways on your hands, moving one hand at a time, while turning the body so that it rotates around in a half circle.

Step 3 Walk back to the starting position. Complete five half circles and returns in each direction.

3

Lying Leg Rotation

This exercise, which is a little harder than it looks, is a great ab-strengthening exercise and is a great workout for your obliques. Try the exercise without the ball first until you get used to it, then add the ball in. It also works your inner thighs (sartotius and pectineus).

TARGET MUSCLES

obliquus externus

pectineus

sartorius

OBLIQUES AND INNER THIGHS

Step 1 Lie on your back, bring your arms out to your side at shoulder width, and bend your legs so that your thighs are perpendicular to your body. Hold your Swiss ball between your knees. Your calves should be parallel to the floor.

Step 2 Press your shoulder blades into the floor and move your legs and the Swiss ball toward your left. Your hips should roll along with your body, but try to keep the rest of your torso on the floor.

Step 3 With your leading knee held as low to the floor as feels comfortable, pause for 5 seconds. Slowly, with control, pull your knees back to your original center position. Pause for another 5 seconds.

Step 4 Repeat the exercise on the other side. Complete 20 repetitions.

CORRECT ACTION
• Keep your thighs perpendicular to your body
• Keep your arms and torso flat on the floor

AVOID
• Fast or jerky movement

TARGET MUSCLES

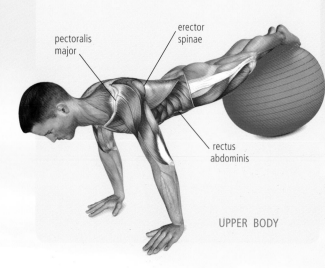

pectoralis major

erector spinae

rectus abdominis

UPPER BODY

Swiss Ball Push-Up

The Swiss Ball Push-Up is a fantastic upper-body strengthening exercise and a highly effective core exercise that improves both power and stabilization in the key core muscles and takes the classic push-up to a greatly increased level of challenge and effectiveness.

Step 1 Begin in a facedown position on your toes with your shins planted on a Swiss ball, and your hands on the floor a little less than shoulder-width apart directly beneath your chest.

Step 2 Start by lowering yourself until your forearms are parallel to the ground, and then push your arms to full extension.

Step 3 Keep your core engaged and your body in a straight line as you lower again. Complete 12 repetitions.

CORRECT ACTION
- Slow and controlled repetitions
- Keep your torso stabilized and your upper body straight
- Keep your hands in line with your chest

AVOID
- Excessive speed
- Shallow or bouncy repetitions

①

②

Hip Crossover

The Hip Crossover helps strengthen and tone the abdominals, and improves core stabilization. All floor exercises are best performed on a yoga or exercise mat.

WARNING Those with lower-back problems should avoid this exercise.

Step 1 Lie on your back, with your arms extended out to your sides. Place your legs on a Swiss ball, with your glutes close to it.

Step 2 Brace your abdominal muscles, and lower your legs to one side, as close to the floor as you can without raising your shoulders off the floor.

Step 3 Return to the starting position, and then switch to the other side. Work up to completing 20 repetitions in each direction.

TARGET MUSCLES

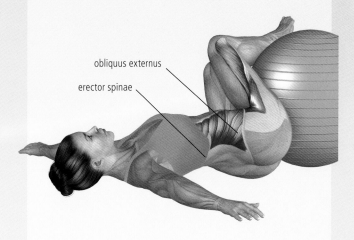

obliquus externus

erector spinae

ABDOMINALS

CORRECT ACTION
• Keep the movement as smooth as possible

AVOID
• Swinging your legs excessively

Medicine Ball Exercises

The medicine ball is an impact-absorbing piece of exercise equipment that can be used to improve your body's core strength, endurance, balance, and coordination. It is used in a wide variety of exercises. They are available in various sizes, from 2 to 25 pounds, and are used to increase explosive power in athletes. They are quite durable and can take a pounding during intense training.

Medicine Ball Throw

The Medicine Ball Throw is a functional movement encompassing rotational drive throughout the core. It is a real-world movement that will build both stamina and core stability. It can also be performed without a partner—go through the same motions, but do not release the ball.

Step 1 Begin in a standing position, holding a medicine ball behind your head.

Step 2 Raise the ball over your head and forward in a sweeping throwing motion and then release the ball to your partner.

Step 3 Receive the returned ball and repeat 20 times.

TARGET MUSCLES

serratus

rectus abdominis

erector spinae

intercostals

obliquus externus

CORE

REAR

FRONT

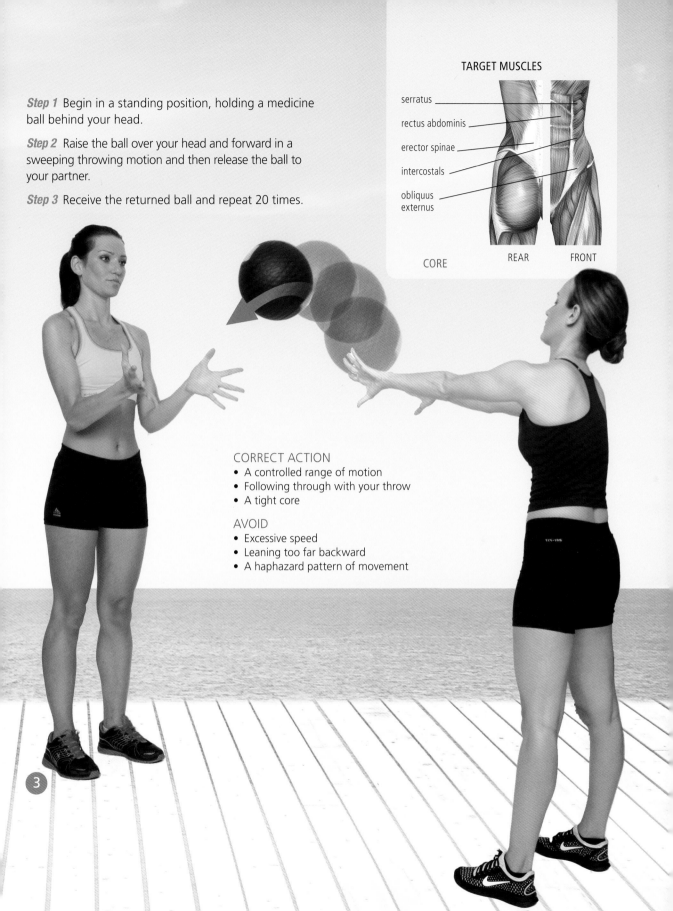

CORRECT ACTION
- A controlled range of motion
- Following through with your throw
- A tight core

AVOID
- Excessive speed
- Leaning too far backward
- A haphazard pattern of movement

3

Big Circles with Medicine Ball

This exercise is an excellent warm-up routine, as well as a precursor to advanced core work to follow later during one's exercise routine. It also doubles as a core strengthener and is an effective means for engaging and readying the frontal core.

Step 1 Begin by standing upright, holding a medicine ball above your head, with your arms straight.

Step 2 Swing your arms downward and to the side, keeping your arms straight all through the movement.

TARGET MUSCLES

erector spinae

serratus

rectus abdominis

intercostals

obliquus externus

REAR   FRONT

CORE

CORRECT ACTION
- Be sure to keep your torso straight throughout the movement
- Keep a tight core throughout

AVOID
- Excessive speed when performing the rotation
- Rounding your back
- A haphazard range of motion

Step 3 Continue swinging the ball to the opposite side and up in a continual 360-degree circular motion.

Step 4 Complete 30 circles, then repeat in the opposite direction for another 30.

Medicine Ball Pullover on a Swiss Ball

This is an exercise that helps keep the upper body stabilized and working cohesively. It is a great workout for the upper back and deltoids. The largest muscle in the back is scientifically known as the latissimus dorsi, often referred to as the "lats." The lats are used any time you pull something. For example, when you open a fridge door, you are primarily using your lat muscles. This, therefore, is a great functional exercise for all such movements.

WARNING Don't do this if you have any shoulder issues.

Step 1 Lie with your head and shoulders supported by a Swiss ball, with your feet on the floor, shoulder-width apart. Hold a medicine ball above your chest, with your arms fully extended.

Step 2 Bend your arms as necessary as you take the ball well behind your head.

Step 3 Straighten your arms as you raise them back into a starting position.

Step 4 Complete three sets of 15 repetitions.

TARGET MUSCLES

triceps brachii

pectoralis minor

pectoralis major

levator scapulae

latissimus dorsi

teres major

deltoideus posterior

TRICEPS

CORRECT ACTION
• Be sure to ease into the exercise

AVOID
• Keeping your arms locked as you stretch behind your head

3

Medicine Ball Push-Up

The Medicine Ball Push-Up is an advanced version of the push-up. Done correctly, this push-up is a highly challenging core exercise. You need to keep your body rigid and in a straight line from head to heels, and not let your hips sag even an inch. This requires using your entire core: abdominals, lower back, and glutes.

TARGET MUSCLES

pectoralis major

triceps brachii

rectus abdominis

multifididus spinae

gluteus maximus

REAR   FRONT

CORE

Step 1 Begin in a push-up position with a medicine ball or block under both hands. Carefully shift your weight forward until your shoulders are positioned directly over your hands and the ball.

Step 2 Lower yourself to the ground as you would in a normal push-up until your chest nearly touches the ball. Keep your torso rigid and your head aligned with your spine.

Step 3 Press upward through your arms. Do not allow your body to sag
or your hips to lift upward. Continue pressing until the arms are fully extended at the elbows.

Step 4 Repeat to failure.

CORRECT ACTION
- Be sure to keep your chest over your hands
- Keep a tight core throughout
- Keep your body in a straight line, head to toe

AVOID
- Excessive speed when performing the rotation
- Allowing your hips to sag

Walk-Over

The Walk-Over resembles the push-up, but targets more muscles in its execution. This is a plyometric exercise that requires both precision and explosive strength. It can be performed with either a medicine ball or a block; here we show a combination of the two—the medicine ball adds a degree of difficulty.

Step 1 Begin in a push-up position with a medicine ball or block under one hand.

Step 2 Lower yourself to the ground as you would in a normal push-up, and as you push upward to arms' length, quickly replace one hand with the other on the medicine ball or block.

Step 3 Switch back and forth between repetitions for 15 repetitions per side.

CORRECT ACTION
• Be sure to keep your chest over your hands
• Keep a tight core throughout

AVOID
• Excessive speed
• Bouncing too much throughout the movement

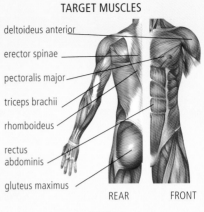

TARGET MUSCLES

deltoideus anterior
erector spinae
pectoralis major
triceps brachii
rhomboideus
rectus abdominis
gluteus maximus

REAR   FRONT

CORE

MODIFICATION

Sit-Up and Throw

The Sit-Up and Throw is an abdominal strengthening exercise that requires the help of a partner. It is a fun and challenging exercise that is a departure from the norm and requires concentration and timing.

Step 1 Begin on your back with your legs bent and your feet firmly planted on the floor. Grasp a medicine ball and hold it in behind your head with both hands.

Step 2 Bring your arms forward while rising off the ground and contracting your abdominals.

Step 3 Throw the ball to your partner.

Step 4 Receive it back, lower, and repeat for 20 repetitions.

TARGET MUSCLES

erector spinae

rectus abdominis

REAR   FRONT

CORE

CORRECT ACTION
- Push through your heels for support
- Lead with your abdominals
- A focused range of motion

AVOID
- Overusing your neck
- Allowing your feet to lift off the ground
- Stressing your lower back

3

Medicine Ball Slam

TARGET MUSCLES

erector spinae

rectus abdominis

deltoideus anterior

hip flexors

gluteus maximus

CORE   REAR   FRONT

The Medicine Ball Slam is an effective means for engaging and readying the frontal core. It is a power movement that involves explosiveness as well as targeting. It is a noisy exercise, best performed on a solid floor.

Step 1 Stand upright, holding a medicine ball behind your head with elbows bent.

Step 2 Swing the ball over your head and throw it straight down with force, squatting as you do so.

Step 3 Catch the ball in the squat position. Stand up and repeat for 20 repetitions.

CORRECT ACTION
- Be sure to keep your torso straight throughout the movement
- Keep a tight core throughout
- Keep your arms bent
- Keep your eyes on the ball

AVOID
- Excessively rounding your back

Power Squat

The Power Squat targets your body's stabilizers, and improves gluteal and thigh strength. It also improves balance and pelvic, trunk, and knee stabilization, at the same time promoting stronger movement patterns.

WARNING Not advisable if you have sharp knee pain, lower-back pain, or shoulder pain.

Step 1 Stand straight, holding a medicine ball in front of your torso.

Step 2 Shift your weight to your left foot, and bend your right knee, lifting your right foot toward your buttocks. Bend your elbows and draw the ball toward your right ear.

Step 3 Maintaining a neutral spine, bend at your hips and knees. Lower your torso toward your left side, bringing the ball toward your right ankle.

Step 4 Press into your left leg and straighten your knees and torso. Return to the starting position. Repeat 15 times for two sets on each leg.

CORRECT ACTION
• The ball should create an arc in the air
• Your hips and knees should be aligned throughout the movement
• Your shoulders and neck must be relaxed

AVOID
• Allowing your knee to extend behind your toes as you bend and rotate
• Moving your foot from its starting position
• Flexing your spine

TARGET MUSCLES

deltoideus posterior
teres minor
erector spinae
gluteus medius
gluteus maximus
rectus femoris
semimembranosus
vastus medialis
gastrocnemius
soleus

GLUTES AND THIGHS

Body Weight Exercises

The obvious benefits of body weight exercises are that they can be done anywhere, and they bypass the need for expensive equipment or a gym membership. Push-ups, dips, squats, mountain climbers, crunches—there is just something unique and special about using one's own body weight for strength purposes that makes these exercises rewarding, challenging, and completely satisfactory.

Step-Down

This a knee-strengthening exercise. It is a challenging movement that will put a lot of strain on your muscles. It can be modified in two ways: changing the height of the step-up box, or changing the speed of the motion. The slower the motion the more difficult the exercise, the higher the box the more difficult the exercise.

WARNING Don't do this if you have any shoulder issues, ankle pain, sharp knee pain, or lower-back pain.

Step 1 Standing up straight on a firm block or step, plant your left foot close to the edge, and allow the right foot to hang off the side. Flex the toes of your right foot.

Step 2 Lift your arms out in front of you for balance, keeping them parallel to the floor. Lower your torso as you bend at your hips and knees, dropping your right leg toward the floor.

Step 3 Without rotating your torso or knee, press upward through your left leg to return to the starting position. Repeat up to 15 times for two sets on each leg.

CORRECT ACTION
- Bend your knee to align with your toes—your knee should not rotate inward
- Your knees and hips move simultaneously as you bend
- Your hips remain behind your foot; lean your torso forward as you lower into the bend

AVOID
- Craning your neck
- Placing weight on the foot being lowered to the floor—only allow a touch

TARGET MUSCLES

gluteus medius
gluteus maximus
vastus intermedius
rectus femoris
semitendinosus
vastus medialis
biceps femoris
vastus lateralis
semimembranosus

KNEES

Tendon Stretch

The Tendon Stretch targets your calf muscles and tendons, and the arches of your feet. As well as lengthening and strengthening the calf muscles, this stretch works your glutes and thighs, and helps improve balance.

Step 1 Standing with your feet together and parallel, extend your arms in front of your body for stability. With your feet planted firmly on the floor, curl your toes upward.

Step 2 Draw in your abdominal muscles, and bend into a squat. Keep your heels planted on the floor and your chest as upright as possible, resisting the urge to bend too far forward.

Step 3 Exhale, returning to the original position. Imagine pressing into the floor as you rise, creating your body's own resistance in your leg muscles. Repeat five to six times.

CORRECT ACTION
- Your chest remains upright
- Your abdominals are pulled in toward your spine
- Your toes curl upward throughout the movement

AVOID
- Allowing your heels to come off the floor
- Rising to the standing position too quickly

TARGET MUSCLES

gluteus maximus

rectus femoris

vastus medialis

biceps femoris

gastrocnemius

tibialis anterior

soleus

adductor hallucis

GROIN

McGill Curl-Up

The McGill Curl-Up works all of your abdominal muscles while keeping your lower back in its naturally arched position. It minimizes stress on your spine while increasing the strength and endurance of the muscles, helping to prevent and relieve lower-back pain. Those with lower-back problems should avoid this exercise.

Step 1 Lie on your back with your right leg fully extended and your left leg bent. Place both hands palm-down underneath your lower back.

Step 2 Keeping your abdominal muscles braced, contract them slightly, bringing your head and shoulders off the floor. Hold for a 5-second count.

Step 3 Lower your head, and repeat for 10 repetitions, then switch legs.

TARGET MUSCLES

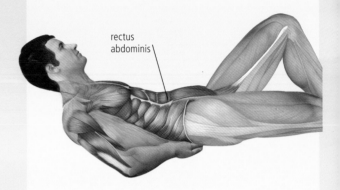

rectus abdominis

ABDOMINALS

CORRECT ACTION
• Raise only your head and upper shoulders during this exercise

AVOID
• Flattening your lower back to the ground

Abdominal Kick-Out

The Abdominal Kick-Out works the rectus abdominis and the deeper transversus abdominis. The exercise improves your posture, stability, and balance, and also increases muscle tone. Core exercises like kick-outs have the added benefit of helping prevent lower-back pain.

WARNING Not advisable if you have neck issues or lower-back pain.

Step 1 Pull your right knee toward your chest and straighten your left leg, raising it to about 45 degrees from the floor.

Step 2 Place your right hand on your right ankle, and your left hand on your right knee (this maintains the proper alignment of the leg).

Step 3 Switch your legs twice, switching your hand placement simultaneously.

Step 4 Switch your legs twice, keeping your hands in their proper placement. Repeat four to six times.

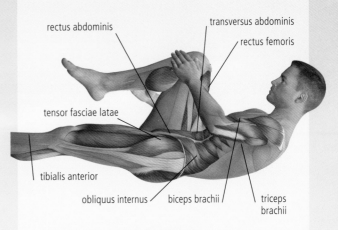

TARGET MUSCLES

rectus abdominis

transversus abdominis

rectus femoris

tensor fasciae latae

tibialis anterior

obliquus internus

biceps brachii

triceps brachii

ABDOMINALS

CORRECT ACTION
- Your outside hand is placed on the ankle of your bent leg, and your inside hand is placed on your bent knee
- The top of your sternum is lifted forward

AVOID
- Allowing your lower back to rise up off the floor
- Using your abdominals to stabilize your core while switching legs

Sit-Up

The Sit-Up is to the abdominals what the bench press is to the pectorals: a highly effective exercise. The iconic Sit-Up is widely used on a daily basis and for good reason: it's the perfect exercise for the rectus abdominis. It is similar to a crunch, but Sit-Ups have a fuller range of motion and condition additional muscles.

Step 1 Begin by lying on your back with your legs bent and your hands behind your head.

Step 2 Start by pushing through your heels for support and raising your trunk off the ground, contracting your abdominals while lifting up toward your knees.

Step 3 Lower and repeat for 20 repetitions.

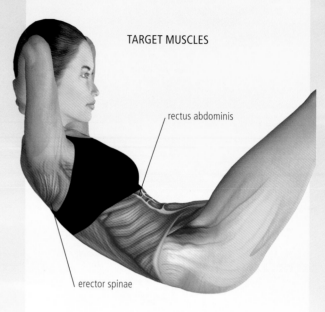

TARGET MUSCLES

rectus abdominis

erector spinae

ABDOMINALS

CORRECT ACTION
- Lead from your belly button
- A controlled lowering
- A precise range of motion

AVOID
- Overusing your neck
- Stressing your lower back
- Swinging upward wildly

Alternating Sit-Up

The Alternating Sit-Up is an advanced variant on the classic Sit-Up that effectively targets the obliques, in addition to the rectus abdominis. It is an exercise upon which the foundation of abdominal and core strength is built.

Step 1 Lie on your back with your legs slightly bent and your hands behind your ears.

Step 2 Push through your heels for support and raise your trunk off the ground.

Step 3 Rotate to the left so your elbow touches your opposite knee, and contract your abdominals.

Step 4 Lower and repeat, rotating to the other side. Perform 15 repetitions per side.

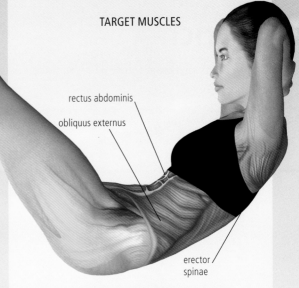

TARGET MUSCLES

rectus abdominis

obliquus externus

erector spinae

ABDOMINALS AND OBLIQUES

CORRECT ACTION
- Lead from your belly button
- A controlled lowering
- A precise and sharp rotation

AVOID
- Overusing your neck
- Stressing your lower back
- Pulling your head too far forward

Crunch

A highly effective abdominal isolator, the Crunch, although shorter in motion than the Sit-Up, places even more tension on the muscles, with less help from ancillary tissues. The difficulty of the Crunch can be increased by lying on a declined bench, placing a weight on the chest, or holding one behind the head. Crunches can also be performed with your hands crossed over your chest.

Step 1 Begin by lying down on your back with your legs bent and your palms placed behind your head with your elbows flared outward.

Step 2 Raise your head and shoulders off the ground while contracting your trunk toward your waist.

Step 3 Keeping your lower back flat to the floor, lower and repeat for up to 40 repetitions.

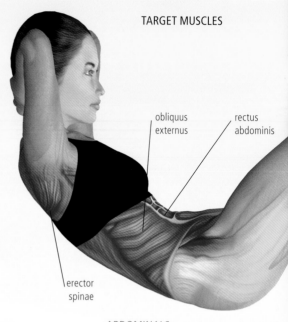

TARGET MUSCLES

obliquus externus

rectus abdominis

erector spinae

ABDOMINALS

CORRECT ACTION
- Maintain a precise and short range of motion
- Tension on the abdominals
- Contract the muscles at the top

AVOID
- Using the neck
- Bouncy and speedy repetitions
- Raising your lower back off the ground

MODIFICATION

Begin by lying supine on the floor with your legs outstretched, and your arms over your head.

Without lifting your legs, lift your arms and torso in a controlled movement.

Continue to curl forward and grasp your feet.

Alternating Crunch

The Alternating Crunch is an advanced version on the regular Crunch that effectively targets the obliques, in addition to the rectus abdominis. As with the Alternating Sit-Up, it is an exercise upon which the foundation of abdominal and core strength is built.

Step 1   Begin by lying down on your back with your legs bent and your palms placed behind your ears with your elbows flared outward.

Step 2   Raise your head and shoulders off the ground while contracting your trunk toward your waist as you rotate your elbow toward the opposite knee.

Step 3   Lower and repeat with the other side for 20 repetitions per side.

CORRECT ACTION
- Lead from your belly button
- A controlled lowering
- A precise and sharp rotation

AVOID
- Overusing your neck
- Stressing your lower back
- Pulling your head too far forward

MODIFICATION

Begin with both feet on the floor. Place the outside of one foot on top of your thigh near your knee.

Reach your opposite elbow toward the knee of your raised leg. After six repetitions, repeat on the other side.

Side Raised-Legs Crunch

The Side Raised-Legs Crunch is a trunk flexion exercise and a variant on the traditional Crunch. Although shorter in motion than the Sit-Up, the Side Raised-Legs Crunch places even more tension on the abdominal and oblique muscles, with less help from ancillary tissues.

Step 1 Lie down on your side with your legs slightly bent, your lower hand on your stomach, and the hand of your upper arm behind your head.

Step 2 Raise your head and shoulders off the ground at the same time as you lift your legs off the ground, keeping your feet together.

Step 3 Lower and repeat for 20 repetitions.

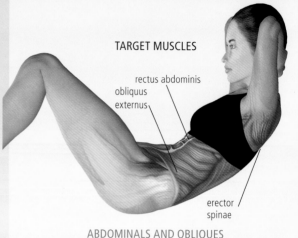

TARGET MUSCLES

rectus abdominis
obliquus externus
erector spinae

ABDOMINALS AND OBLIQUES

CORRECT ACTION
• Maintain a precise range of motion
• Tension on the abdominals
• Keep your feet together

AVOID
• Using the neck
• Bouncy and speedy repetitions

Double-Leg Ab Press

Pressing as hard as you can against your quadriceps is a great workout for your core muscles. If this is too difficult, the exercise can be modified by pressing on one leg at a time.

WARNING Not advisable if you have back pain or hip pain.

Step 1 Lie on your back with your knees and feet lifted in tabletop position, your thighs making a 90-degree angle with your upper body. Place your hands on the front of your knees, your fingers facing upward, one palm on each leg.

Step 2 Flex your feet and, keeping your elbows bent and pulled into your sides, press your hands into your knees. Create resistance by pushing back against your hands with your knees. Hold for up to one minute, and repeat five times.

TARGET MUSCLES

vastus lateralis
vastus intermedius
rectus femoris
triceps brachii
iliacus
iliopsoas
rectus abdominis
transversus abdominis

CORE

CORRECT ACTION
- Your elbows are pulled in toward your sides
- Your shoulders and neck remain relaxed
- Your feet are flexed and your knees pressed together
- Your tailbone is tucked up toward the ceiling

AVOID
- Holding your breath while performing the exercise

Lemon Squeezer

If you need to take your abdominal workout to a higher intensity, try a Lemon Squeezer, in which you visualize an imaginary lemon on your stomach that you must squeeze by raising your legs and torso off the ground while contracting your abdominal muscles.

WARNING Not advisable if you have lower-back pain.

Step 1 Lie supine on the floor. Lift your legs, head, neck, and shoulders slightly off the floor, being careful not to arch your lower back. Your arms should be raised and parallel to the floor.

Step 2 Pause at the top of the movement, and then lower yourself almost to the starting position.

Step 3 Repeat the motion without completely lying down on the mat. Repeat 15 times for two sets.

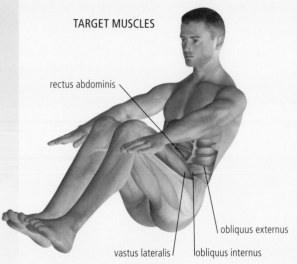

TARGET MUSCLES

rectus abdominis

obliquus externus

vastus lateralis

obliquus internus

ABDOMINALS

CORRECT ACTION
• The chin remains tucked
• Your thigh muscles are firm throughout the exercise

AVOID
• Allowing your shoulders to lift up toward your ears

Chair Abdominal Crunch

Chair workouts are great for anyone who spends a lot of time at a desk, and for older people who can benefit from the added stability a chair offers. Because your abdominals are a group of smaller, linked muscles, they benefit from daily workouts, and rarely require a day of rest between.

WARNING Not advisable if you have lower-back pain.

Step 1 Sit on a chair with your hands grasping the sides of the seat and your arms straight.

Step 2 Tuck your torso forward and lift your buttocks slightly off the chair, while swinging your legs up. Your hips and knees should be bent to form 90-degree angles.

Step 3 Tuck your tailbone toward the front of the chair, and bend your knees toward your chest. Bend your elbows simultaneously. Extend your elbows and press through your shoulders.

Step 4 Keeping your head in a neutral position, press into the chair and lower your legs to return to the starting position. Repeat 15 times for two sets.

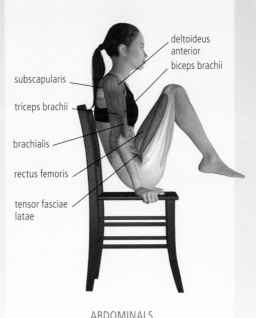

TARGET MUSCLES

deltoideus anterior
biceps brachii
subscapularis
triceps brachii
brachialis
rectus femoris
tensor fasciae latae

ABDOMINALS

CORRECT ACTION
• Your spine is neutral as you progress through the motion
• Your knees align over your ankles
• Your body remains close to the chair

AVOID
• Allowing your shoulders to lift up toward your ears

1

2

Oblique Roll-Down

This exercise is used for strengthening your core and helps develop the muscles to do more advanced exercises. It targets the obliques and abdominals while increasing your ability to maintain core stability.

WARNING Not advisable if you have a herniated disk.

TARGET MUSCLES

rectus abdominis

transversus abdominis

obliquus externus

obliquus internus

ABDOMINALS AND OBLIQUES

Step 1 Sit with your arms extended to the sides, parallel to the floor.

Step 2 Contract your abdominals, drawing your navel to your spine and lengthening the spine upward.

Step 3 Roll backward while simultaneously rotating your torso to one side.

Step 4 Maintaining spinal flexion, rotate your torso back to the center.

Step 5 Rotate to the other side, deepening the abdominal contraction.

Step 6 Return back to the center, and repeat the sequence four to six times on each side.

CORRECT ACTION
- Your arms lengthen as you roll down to create opposition throughout the torso
- Your neck is relaxed and lengthened to prevent straining
- Your spine is articulated while rolling up and down

AVOID
- Tensing your neck and shoulder muscles

①

②

Quadruped Lateral Lift

This exercise primarily targets the erector spinae muscles, which run along your spine and are responsible for extending your torso. Your glutes assist in the movement, driving your leg backward.

WARNING Not advisable if you have sharp back pain or wrist pain.

Step 1 Kneel on your hands and knees, your spine in neutral position.

Step 2 Keep your weight centered and raise your right knee—still bent—out to the side.

Step 3 Raise and lower your leg without moving your hips. Repeat ten times, and then switch legs.

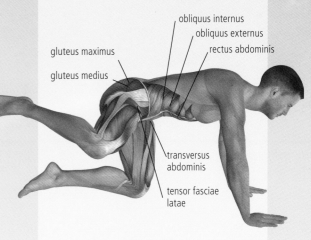

TARGET MUSCLES

obliquus internus
obliquus externus
rectus abdominis
gluteus maximus
gluteus medius
transversus abdominis
tensor fasciae latae

ERECTOR SPINAE AND GLUTES

CORRECT ACTION
- Your spine remains neutral, so as to prevent the lower back from sagging
- Your chin remains tucked and your head in neutral
- Your hands press into the floor and out of the shoulders to keep the shoulders from sinking near the ears

AVOID
- Lifting the hip as you lift your leg

Abdominal Hip Lift

The Abdominal Hip Lift strengthens the rectus abdominis (the muscle between the ribs and hips) and the obliques. Try to work up to two sets of 10 to 12 repetitions, with a short break between. This is a very good exercise for improving the strength of your lower abdominal muscles.

Step 1 Lie down with your legs in the air and crossed at the ankles, knees straight. Place your arms on the floor, straight by your sides.

Step 2 Pinching your legs together and squeezing your buttocks, press into the back of your arms to lift your hips upward.

Step 3 Slowly return your hips to the floor. Repeat ten times, then switch with the opposite leg crossed in the front.

TARGET MUSCLES

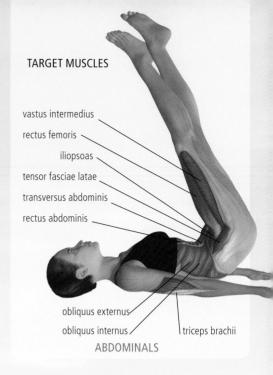

- vastus intermedius
- rectus femoris
- iliopsoas
- tensor fasciae latae
- transversus abdominis
- rectus abdominis
- obliquus externus
- obliquus internus
- triceps brachii

ABDOMINALS

CORRECT ACTION
- Your legs remain straight and firm throughout the exercise
- Your neck and shoulders are relaxed as you lift the hips

AVOID
- Jerking your movements or using momentum to lift the hips

MODIFICATION

Keeping your hips on the floor, raise your arms toward the ceiling. Reach toward your toes as you lift your shoulders off the floor.

Hand Walkout

The Hand Walkout builds strength in your anterior core and lats very quickly. It trains the abdominals isometrically and is an excellent alternative to the ab-wheel rollout. Since it requires no equipment, you can do it anywhere.

Step 1 Stand straight, arms at your sides.

Step 2 Bend forward from the waist, and place your hands on the floor in front of you, at a distance slightly wider than your feet. Keep your knees as straight as possible.

Step 3 Walk slowly forward on your hands, one "step" at a time, as far as you can—ideally to a full plank position.

Step 4 Return by walking back toward the starting position and pushing your hips upward, folding the torso at the hips.

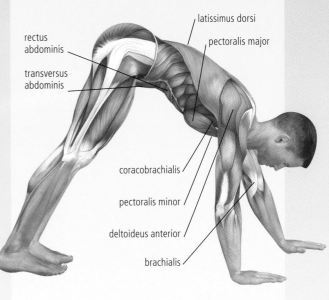

TARGET MUSCLES

- latissimus dorsi
- rectus abdominis
- pectoralis major
- transversus abdominis
- coracobrachialis
- pectoralis minor
- deltoideus anterior
- brachialis

CORE

CORRECT ACTION
- Your spine and legs remain straight
- A controlled, steady movement

AVOID
- Bending your knees
- Allowing your spine to sag in the middle
- Bending your elbows

Kneeling Side Kick

The Kneeling Side Kick is a great exercise to help tighten your buttocks. It will strengthen and tone your seat muscles with a special focus on the gluteus medius (which is the smallest of the glute muscles). Having strong glutes will also help ensure healthy and balanced movement patterns.

WARNING Not advisable if you have wrist issues, severe back pain, or shoulder issues.

Step 1 Kneel with your right hand on the floor directly below your shoulder, with the fingers pointing outward. Place your left hand behind your head. Lift your left leg to the height of your hip and straighten it, reaching out of your heel.

Step 2 Pull your left leg behind you, flexing your foot. Try not to move at your waist. Keep your whole body aligned in one plane so that there is no rotation.

Step 3 Kick your left leg straight out in front of you, pointing your toes and keeping the leg at hip height. Repeat the sequence ten times on each side.

TARGET MUSCLES

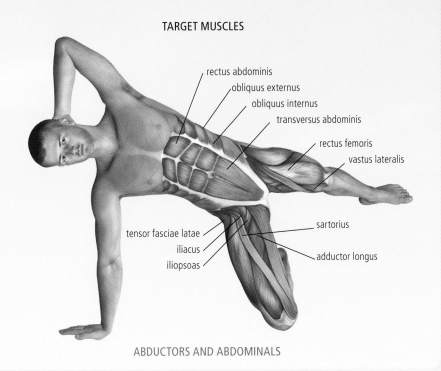

- rectus abdominis
- obliquus externus
- obliquus internus
- transversus abdominis
- rectus femoris
- vastus lateralis
- tensor fasciae latae
- iliacus
- iliopsoas
- sartorius
- adductor longus

ABDUCTORS AND ABDOMINALS

CORRECT ACTION

- Bear your weight on the palm of your hand to help maintain balance
- Your neck remains long and relaxed
- Your body aligns so that your shoulders, hips, and legs line up to better activate deep muscles

AVOID

- Wobbling when moving the leg—instead, make the movement smaller

Thigh Rock-Back

The Thigh Rock-Back is a simple but effective exercise that improves abdominal and thigh strength. Those with lower-back problems should avoid this exercise.

Step 1 Begin in a kneeling position, with a straight back and your arms at your sides.

Step 2 Lean back while keeping your body in a straight line and your abdominals contracted.

Step 3 While still leaning back, flex your glute muscles, then slowly return to the starting position. Complete 10 repetitions.

CORRECT ACTION
• Maintain a straight line with your torso
• Move slowly through the motion
• Contract your abdominals as you lean back

AVOID
• Leaning back too far

TARGET MUSCLES

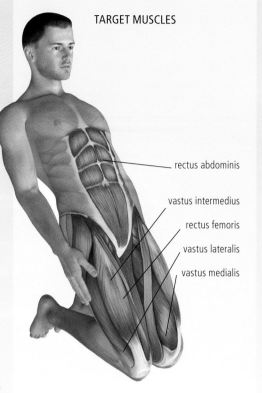

rectus abdominis

vastus intermedius

rectus femoris

vastus lateralis

vastus medialis

ABDOMINALS AND THIGHS

Standing Knee Crunch

It is important to do standing abdominal exercises to improve strength and stability. The Standing Knee Crunch strengthens the core, calves, and gluteal muscles as well as improving balance.

Step 1 Standing tall with your left leg in front of the right, extend your hands up toward the ceiling, your arms straight. Shift your weight onto your left foot, and raise your right knee to the height of your hips.

Step 2 Simultaneously go up on the toes of your left leg, while pulling your elbows down by your sides, your hands making fists. This creates the crunch.

Step 3 Pause at the top of the movement, and then return to the starting position. Repeat the sequence with your right leg as the standing leg. Repeat ten times on each leg.

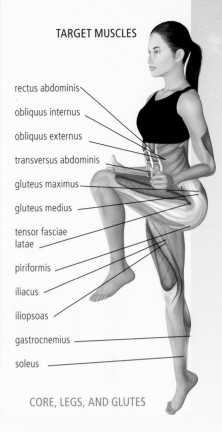

TARGET MUSCLES

rectus abdominis

obliquus internus

obliquus externus

transversus abdominis

gluteus maximus

gluteus medius

tensor fasciae latae

piriformis

iliacus

iliopsoas

gastrocnemius

soleus

CORE, LEGS, AND GLUTES

CORRECT ACTION
- Your standing leg is straight as you raise up on your toes
- Your shoulders are relaxed as you pull your arms down for the crunch
- Flex the toes of your raised leg

AVOID
- Tilting forward as you switch legs

1

2

Bridge

The Bridge exercise functions as a core strengthener, a back bend, and enhances core stability. In yoga, the pose is called Setu Bandha Sarvangasana. In Pilates it is simply called the Bridge. To perform the Bridge exercise correctly, you need to keep your body in proper alignment.

Step 1 Begin on your back with your legs bent, your feet flat on the ground, and your arms extended on the floor, parallel to your body.

Step 2 Push through your heels while raising your pelvis until your torso is aligned with your thighs. Hold for 30 seconds, then lower yourself back down. Perform three repetitions.

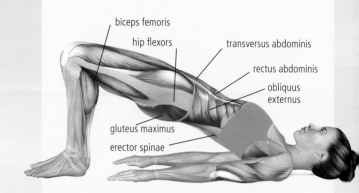

TARGET MUSCLES

biceps femoris

hip flexors

transversus abdominis

rectus abdominis

obliquus externus

gluteus maximus

erector spinae

CORE

CORRECT ACTION
• Push through your heels, not your toes

AVOID
• Overextending your abdominals past your thighs in the finished position

Bridge with Leg Lift

This exercise works your abdominals, back, and buttocks. It also improves your balance. The exercise can be simplified by decreasing the range of motion—just raise your foot slightly off the floor. If necessary, prop yourself up with your hands beneath your hips once you are in the bridge position.

WARNING Not advisable if you have neck issues or a knee injury.

Step 1 Lie in supine position on the floor, your arms by your sides and lengthened toward your feet. Your legs should be bent, with your feet flat on the floor. Lift your hips and spine off the floor, creating one long line from your knees to your shoulders. Keep your weight shifted over your feet.

Step 2 Keeping your legs bent, bring your left knee toward your chest. Lower your left leg until your toe touches the mat. Be sure to keep your pelvis level.

Step 3 Bring your left knee toward your chest again. Repeat sequence four to five times. Lower your left leg to the floor, switch legs, and repeat the exercise with your right leg. Repeat sequence four to five times.

TARGET MUSCLES

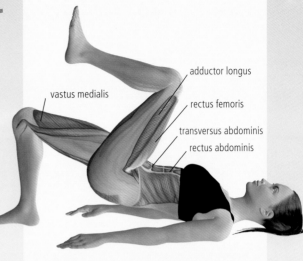

vastus medialis

adductor longus

rectus femoris

transversus abdominis

rectus abdominis

ABDOMINALS, BACK, AND GLUTES

CORRECT ACTION
- Your hips and torso remain stable throughout the exercise
- Your buttocks remain tightly squeezed as you scoop in your abdominals for stability

AVOID
- Allowing your back to do the work by extending out of your hips
- Lifting your hips so high that your weight shifts onto your neck

V-Up

V-Ups are a challenging means of isolating the rectus abdominis through an entire range of motion. They are an effective core-strengthening exercise. Timing and precision are important components for maximizing effectiveness.

Step 1   Begin by lying on your back. Simultaneously raise both your legs and lift your torso, reaching your arms forward until they are nearly touching your feet.

Step 2 Maintain a flat back and try to form a perfect V shape with your torso and legs. Lower and repeat for 25 repetitions.

TARGET MUSCLES

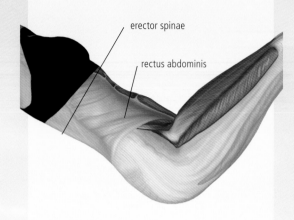

erector spinae

rectus abdominis

ABDOMINALS

CORRECT ACTION
- Keep both your arms and legs straight
- A controlled lowering
- A precise range of motion

AVOID
- Overusing your neck
- Stressing your lower back
- Swinging upward wildly

Scissors

This exercise improves core stability, and increases abdominal strength and endurance. It can be modified by performing all the repetitions on one leg before switching to the other. Those with tight hamstrings should avoid this exercise.

Step 1 Lie with your back on the floor, your arms by your sides, and your legs raised in a tabletop position.

Step 2 Inhale, drawing in your abdominals. Reach your legs straight up, and lift your head and shoulders off the floor. Hold the position while lengthening your legs.

Step 3 Stretching your right leg away from your body, raise your left leg toward your trunk. Hold your left calf with your hands, pulsing twice while keeping your shoulders down.

Step 4 Repeat the motion with your right leg raised and your left leg stretched away.

TARGET MUSCLES

rectus femoris

biceps femoris

rectus abdominis

ABDOMINALS AND LEGS

CORRECT ACTION
• Keep your pelvis stabilized and your spine straight

AVOID
• Overextending your raised leg

Leg Raises

Leg Raises are a good abdominal strengthener for what is commonly cited as the "lower abdominals"—although this label is false, as the rectus abdominis is one muscle and not sectionalized. It is felt particularly below the navel.

Step 1 Begin by lying on your back with your arms at your sides and your legs outstretched with toes pointed and your heels elevated just off the ground.

Step 2 Raise both legs until they are nearly at a 90-degree angle to the ground.

Step 3 Lower your legs to just short of the ground and repeat for 25 repetitions.

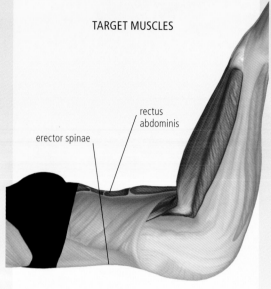

TARGET MUSCLES

rectus abdominis

erector spinae

ABDOMINALS

CORRECT ACTION
• Keep your upper body braced
• A controlled lowering
• A precise range of motion

AVOID
• Letting your legs touch the ground
• Stressing your lower back
• Swinging with momentum

Single-Leg Circles

The Single-Leg Circle is one of the best exercises for testing your core strength. The abdominal muscles must work hard to keep the shoulders and pelvis stable despite the movement of the leg. This exercise also tones and stretches the thighs.

Step 1 Lie flat on the floor, with both legs and arms extended. Bend your right knee toward your chest, and then straighten your leg up in the air. Anchor the rest of your body to the floor, straightening both knees and pressing your shoulders back and down.

Step 2 Cross your raised leg up and over your body, aiming for your left shoulder. Continue making a circle with the raised leg, returning to the center. Add emphasis to the motion by pausing at the top between repetitions.

Step 3 Switch directions so that you aim your leg away from your body. Repeat with the other leg. Complete the full movement five to eight times.

TARGET MUSCLES

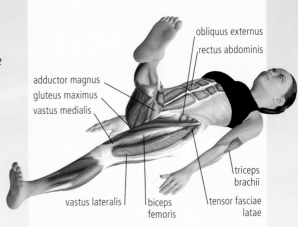

obliquus externus
rectus abdominis
adductor magnus
gluteus maximus
vastus medialis
triceps brachii
vastus lateralis
biceps femoris
tensor fasciae latae

ABDOMINALS AND THIGHS

CORRECT ACTION
- Your hips and torso remain stable while your legs are mobilized
- Your raised leg is elongated from your hip through your foot

AVOID
- Making your leg circles too big to maintain stability

Front Plank

The Front Plank is a classic exercise that increases ability to support your own body weight. It is not advisable for pregnant women. Primary emphasis is on the rectus abdominis and erector spinae. As a more challenging modification, instead of resting on your forearms, extend your arms fully when on all fours and then continue with step 2.

Step 1 Position yourself on all fours, then plant your forearms on the floor parallel to one another, with 90-degree bends at the elbows.

Step 2 Raise your knees off the ground, and lengthen your legs until they are in line with your body. Hold for 30 seconds (building up to 2 minutes).

CORRECT ACTION
• Keep your abdominal muscles tight and your body in a straight line

AVOID
• Bridging too high, since this can take stress off the working muscles

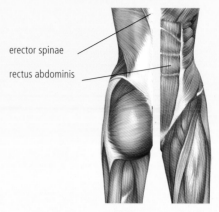

TARGET MUSCLES

erector spinae

rectus abdominis

REAR   FRONT

ABDOMINALS AND ERECTOR SPINAE

1

2

Plank-Ups

Plank-Ups are an advanced building-block core exercise expanding upon the basic Plank position. This is a taxing, repetitious, and highly effective movement.

Step 1 Begin on an exercise mat on all fours in a prone position. Plant your forearms on the ground parallel to one another, raise your knees off the ground, and lengthen your legs until they are in line with your arms and your toes are touching the ground.

Step 2 Replace one planted forearm with one hand extended to full lockout position, then repeat with the other arm until in a completed push-up position. Reverse one arm at a time, going from planted hand to forearm until back in the initial plank position, for 15 repetitions.

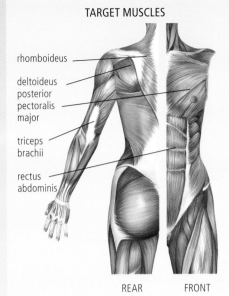

TARGET MUSCLES

rhomboideus

deltoideus posterior

pectoralis major

triceps brachii

rectus abdominis

REAR   FRONT

ABDOMINALS AND ERECTOR SPINAE

CORRECT ACTION
- Keep your body braced
- Planting each hand
- A precise range of motion

AVOID
- Stressing your wrists
- Sudden crashing down
- Excess momentum

1

2

Plank Roll-Down

The Plank Roll-Down is a challenging exercise that targets your pectoral muscles and upper-arm muscles. Another benefit is that it helps to stabilize the core, and works to strengthen your abdominals.

WARNING Not advisable if you have wrist pain, shoulder issues, or lower-back pain.

Step 1 Stand tall with your weight equally distributed between your feet.

Step 2 Relaxing your neck, bend from your waist and bring your hands down toward the floor. Place them in front of your feet so that they are flat on the floor.

Step 3 Walk your hands away from your feet until your body reaches a plank position, forming a straight line from your shoulders to your heels.

Step 4 Keeping your arms straight, dip your shoulders three times while maintaining the plank position.

Step 5 Walk your hands back to your feet and return to an upright position. Repeat ten times at a rapid pace.

CORRECT ACTION
- Your spine and legs remain straight
- A slow, steady movement
- Your abdominals remain up and tensed

AVOID
- Bending your knees or spine
- Allowing your elbows to bend

TARGET MUSCLES

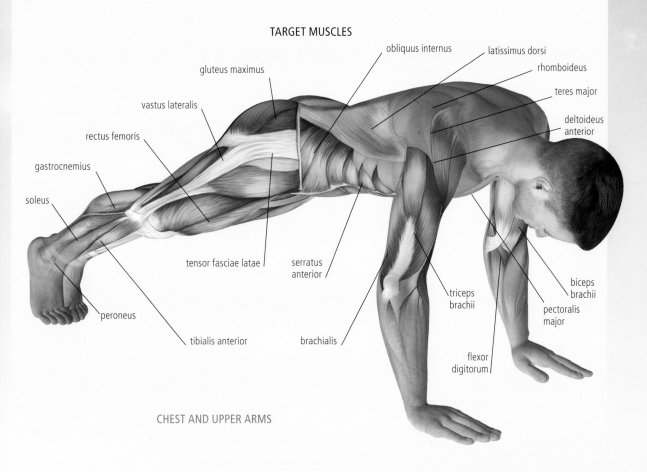

obliquus internus

latissimus dorsi

rhomboideus

teres major

deltoideus anterior

gluteus maximus

vastus lateralis

rectus femoris

gastrocnemius

soleus

tensor fasciae latae

serratus anterior

triceps brachii

biceps brachii

pectoralis major

peroneus

tibialis anterior

brachialis

flexor digitorum

CHEST AND UPPER ARMS

MODIFICATION

Roll down to a plank position on your elbows, rather than on your hands.

Supporting your torso with your forearms and maintaining the plank position, dip up and down three times.

Knee-Pull Plank

The Knee-Pull Plank is a great exercise that requires no equipment, so you can do it anywhere you go. The aim of the exercise is to build core strength. Your abdominals will get a good workout, and the exercise will also help build strength and endurance in your upper body. Keep the movements slow and precise.

WARNING Not advisable if you have wrist pain, shoulder issues, or lower-back pain.

Step 1 Begin by assuming a standard plank position.

Step 2 Draw your left knee into your chest while leaning forward and flexing your foot. Your right leg should be up on its toes.

Step 3 Extend your right leg through the heel and rock your body back, shifting your weight into your left foot.

Step 4 Drop your head between your arms and straighten and raise your left leg toward the ceiling. Repeat the entire exercise 10 times per leg.

TARGET MUSCLES

biceps femoris
vastus lateralis
rectus femoris
rectus abdominis
vastus medialis
obliquus externus
semimembranosus
gastrocnemius

CORE, HAMSTRINGS, GLUTES, AND SCAPULAR AREA

CORRECT ACTION
• Keep your body in a straight line throughout the exercise

AVOID
• Bending the knee of the supporting leg

Reverse Plank

The Reverse Plank exercise is an often-overlooked core exercise. This exercise isolates and strengthens the gluteus muscles and hamstrings. Done correctly, it engages both the abdominals and the lower-back muscles. The Reverse Plank can also be used as a rehab exercise to improve core and spinal stabilization.

WARNING Not advisable if you have wrist pain, shoulder issues, or lower-back pain.

Step 1 Sit with your legs extended in front of you and your arms directly behind you, with your fingers pointing straight ahead.

Step 2 Push through your palms and raise your hips and glutes off the ground until your body forms a straight line from the shoulders.

Step 3 Raise one leg and hold for 30 seconds, then switch legs.

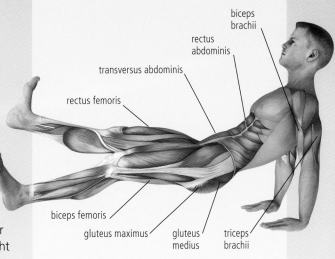

TARGET MUSCLES

biceps brachii
rectus abdominis
transversus abdominis
rectus femoris
biceps femoris
gluteus maximus
gluteus medius
triceps brachii

CORE, HAMSTRINGS, AND GLUTES

CORRECT ACTION
- Keep your pelvis elevated for the duration of the exercise

AVOID
- Letting your shoulders slouch backward

Side-Bend Plank

The Side-Bend Plank is a great exercise for beginning exercisers. Increasing the amount of time spent performing the basic side plank will greatly increase its intensity. You'll be suprised at how a few extra seconds can make this exercise much more difficult!

WARNING Not advisable if you have wrist pain, shoulder issues, or lower-back pain.

Step 1 Lie on your right side with one arm supporting your torso, aligning the wrist under your shoulder. Place your left arm on top of your left leg. Your legs should be strongly squeezed together in adduction, with legs parallel and feet flexed. Draw your navel toward your spine.

Step 2 Press into the palm of your right hand and lift your hips off the floor, creating a straight line between your heels and head.

Step 3 Hold until failure, then repeat on the other arm.

TARGET MUSCLES

transversus abdominis

erector spinae

deltoideus anterior

TRUNK AND SHOULDERS

MODIFICATION

Rather than supporting your torso with your arm straight, bend your elbow so that it is aligned below your shoulder.

Press into your forearm to lift your body into the side plank position.

CORRECT ACTION
• Keep your body in a straight line throughout the exercise

AVOID
• Bending the knee of the supporting leg

Tiny Steps

This exercise targets your glutes and thigh muscles, and also works your abdominals. It is a simple routine that increases in effectiveness through duration—the longer you can perform it, the better.

WARNING Not advisable if you have wrist pain, shoulder issues, or lower-back pain.

Step 1 Lie in supine position with your knees bent and feet flat on the floor.

Step 2 Place your hands on your hip bones to feel if you are moving your hips from side to side.

Step 3 Raise your right knee to your chest while pulling your navel toward your spine. Hold the position at the top.

Step 4 As you continue to pull your navel toward your spine, lower your right leg onto the floor while controlling any movement in your hips.

Step 5 Alternate legs to complete the full movement. Repeat as many times as you can manage.

TARGET MUSCLES

biceps femoris

rectus femoris

gluteus maximus

obliquus internus

tensor fasciae latae

GLUTES AND THIGHS

CORRECT ACTION
- Your navel is pulled in toward your spine throughout the exercise

AVOID
- Allowing your hips to move back and forth while legs are mobilized

Advanced Superman

This medium-intensity exercise strengthens your core muscles and lower back by isolating them as you lift your legs and shoulders. To make the exercise less challenging, stretch your arms out in front (the Superman), or alternatively you can place a pillow under your head to decrease the amount you must lift.

WARNING Not advisable if you have wrist pain, shoulder issues, or lower-back pain.

Step 1 Lie facedown. Bend your elbows, placing your hands behind your ears. Extend your legs and press down into the floor with your thighs and the tops of your feet.

Step 2 Inhaling, lift your chest and legs off the floor.

Step 3 Hold for 15 to 30 seconds.

Step 4 On an exhalation, lower yourself to the floor.

CORRECT ACTION
• Keep your body in a straight line throughout the exercise

AVOID
• Bending the knees
• Overarching your back

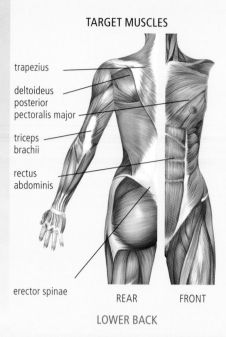

TARGET MUSCLES

trapezius
deltoideus posterior
pectoralis major
triceps brachii
rectus abdominis
erector spinae

REAR   FRONT

LOWER BACK

Prone Heel Beats

Prone Heel Beats are an effective Pilates movement that engage the abdominals, inner thighs, and glutes to help shape and create firm buttocks. It is one of the best glute exercises you can do on the mat. The main thing you have to remember is to keep your abdominal muscles pulled in and to go for length along your back and down the back of your legs so that you protect your lower back.

WARNING Not advisable if you have wrist pain, shoulder issues, or lower-back pain.

Step 1 Begin by lying facedown with your arms at your sides, slightly elevated and head raised back.

Step 2 Lift your legs and part them slightly, turning your feet slightly outward.

Step 3 Beat your heels together 20 times.

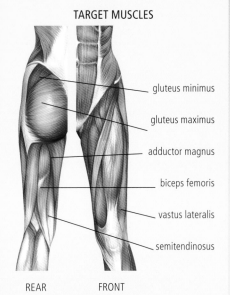

TARGET MUSCLES

gluteus minimus

gluteus maximus

adductor magnus

biceps femoris

vastus lateralis

semitendinosus

REAR   FRONT

ABDOMINALS AND GLUTES

CORRECT ACTION
- Legs elevated throughout the movement
- Draw your abdominals in toward your spine
- A controlled motion

AVOID
- Overengaging your shoulders
- Sloppy form
- An improper setup

Mountain Climber

The Mountain Climber is a stability exercise that also tests and extends the endurance and the activation of many muscles working together to execute the movement. This is a taxing and repetitious exercise that, quite simply, works.

WARNING Not advisable if you have wrist pain, shoulder issues, or lower-back pain.

Step 1 Begin in a completed Push-Up position with your body maintained in a straight line.

Step 2 Raise one leg and bring your knee as close to your chest as able, then return to the starting position.

Step 3 Repeat with the other leg, alternating both for 30 seconds to 2 minutes.

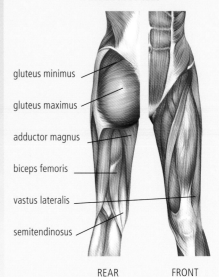

TARGET MUSCLES

gluteus minimus

gluteus maximus

adductor magnus

biceps femoris

vastus lateralis

semitendinosus

REAR   FRONT

THIGHS

CORRECT ACTION
- Keep a tight core throughout the movement
- Breathe throughout the exercise
- Be light on your toes

AVOID
- Your toes hitting the ground excessively hard
- Holding your breath

Push-Up

A basic Push-Up is one of the most effective ways to strengthen your chest and arm muscles. There are literally dozens of variations of the Push-Up, but simple Push-Ups require no equipment other than your own body weight, and they can be done anywhere there is a flat surface with enough space for you to stretch out.

Step 1 Stand straight, inhale, and pull your navel to your spine.

Step 2 Exhale as you roll down one vertebra at a time until your hands touch the floor in front of you.

Step 3 Walk your hands out until they are directly beneath your shoulders in the plank position.

Step 4 Inhale, and set your body by drawing your abdominals to your spine. Squeeze your buttocks and legs together and stretch out of your heels, bringing your body into a straight line.

Step 5 Exhale and inhale as you bend your elbows and lower your body toward the floor. Then push upward to return to the plank position. Keep your elbows close to your body. Repeat until failure.

TARGET MUSCLES

- trapezius
- deltoideus posterior
- pectoralis major
- pectoralis minor
- triceps brachii
- coracobrachialis
- rectus abdominis
- transversus abdominis
- obliquus externus
- obliquus internus

FRONT   REAR

CHEST AND ARMS

CORRECT ACTION
- Your neck remains long and relaxed as you perform the exercise
- Your buttocks remain tightly squeezed as you scoop in your abdominals for stability

AVOID
- Allowing your shoulders to lift toward your ears
- Bending the knees

2

5

Chair Pose

The Chair Pose is a standing yoga posture that tones the entire body, particularly the thighs. It can be a challenging pose for your thighs and it gets your heart pumping quickly. The Chair Pose builds strength and stamina throughout the whole body.

WARNING Not advisable if you have wrist pain, shoulder issues, or lower-back pain.

Step 1 Start by standing in an upright position.

Step 2 Raise your arms over your head, bend your knees, and extend your upper body forward to a 45-degree angle.

Step 3 Keep your feet flat, and push through your heels. Hold for 30–60 seconds.

TARGET MUSCLES

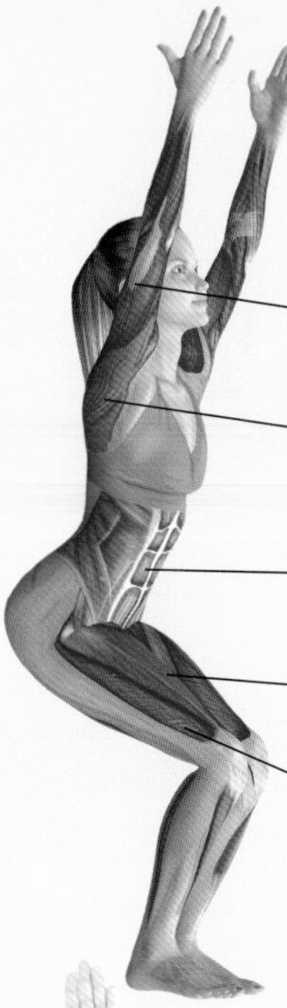

triceps brachii

deltoideus posterior

vastus intermedius

rectus femoris

vastus lateralis

THIGHS AND ARMS

CORRECT ACTION
• Keep your abdominals contracted throughout the exercise

AVOID
• Avoid arching your back excessively

1

2

Side-Lift Bend

The Side-Lift Bend is a challenging move for core endurance and shoulder girdle endurance. It targets your obliques and quadratus lumborum. The exercise can also be performed with your arm outstreched in line with your torso.

WARNING Not advisable if you have wrist pain, shoulder issues, or lower-back pain.

Step 1 Lie on your left side with your right arm placed behind your head and your left arm lying flat on top of your thigh. Tightly press your legs together.

Step 2 Tighten your abdominals and lift both legs off the floor.

Step 3 Sliding your right hand down your outstretched leg, lift your head and crunch your oblique muscles from your upper body and lower body simultaneously. Repeat 10 times on each side.

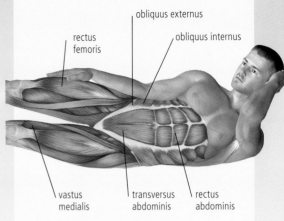

TARGET MUSCLES

obliquus externus

rectus femoris

obliquus internus

vastus medialis

transversus abdominis

rectus abdominis

ABDOMINALS AND THIGHS

CORRECT ACTION
• Squeeze your buttocks before lifting to better stabilize the pelvis
• Elongate your neck
• Your hand slides down on the top leg as you crunch up

AVOID
• Stressing your neck

Quadruped

The Quadruped is a core stability exercise that calls for many muscles to work together in order to perform the movement. It can be made more difficult by starting from the upper part of a push-up position. The Quadruped is an effective exercise for developing the core and lower back. Extension of the shoulders and hips means that it gives both upper and lower body parts a great workout while improving overall coordination and balance.

Step 1 Begin on all fours with your hands, knees, and feet shoulder-width apart.

Step 2 Start by fully extending one leg while straightening the opposite arm in front. Hold the position for 10 seconds, contracting your abs and tensing your thigh muscles. Try to keep as still as possible.

Step 3 Return to the start position.

Step 4 Perform 20 repetitions and then proceed to the other side.

CORRECT ACTION
• Your knees are bent 90 degrees at the start
• Draw your abdominals in toward your spine
• Keep your back flat

AVOID
• Overengaging your wrists
• Sloppy form
• Firing muscles at different times

TARGET MUSCLES

biceps femoris

adductor magnus

obliquus internus

ABDOMINALS AND THIGHS

MODIFICATION

Instead of kneeling, press into a plank position to begin, and then raise the opposite arm and leg.

2

Clamshell Series

The Clamshell Series is a simple and effective exercise for abdominal stabilization as well as for working the abductors and adductors; it also results in increased pelvic stability. This exercise targets the muscles of your glutes and hamstrings, producing a good amount of gluteus medius and gluteus maximus activity, especially if your technique is good. The exercise can be made more challenging by adding a resistance band around your knees.

Step 1 Begin on your side with your knees together, leaning on your forearm, with the other hand on the floor in front of you, or resting on your hip.

Step 2 Bend your top leg slightly and start by opening your top leg while keeping the spine straight and the body stable. Open and close your legs 10 times, keeping your feet together.

Step 3 Raise your ankles off the floor. Open and close your legs 10 times, keeping your feet together.

Step 4 Repeat with the opposite leg.

CORRECT ACTION
- Keep your spine straight throughout the movement
- A controlled range of motion
- Keep your feet in contact with one another

AVOID
- Allowing your hips to raise while lifting your knees
- A haphazard motion

1

TARGET MUSCLES

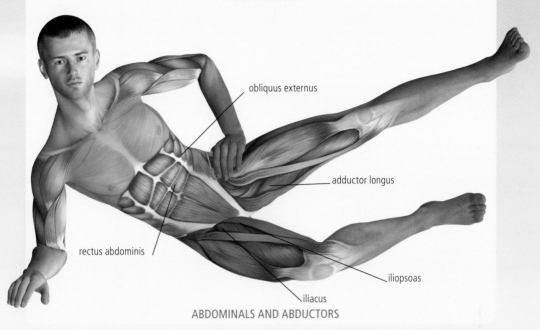

obliquus externus

adductor longus

rectus abdominis

iliopsoas

iliacus

ABDOMINALS AND ABDUCTORS

3

Hand-to-Toe Lift

The Hand-to-Toe Lift is a challenging exercise that will increase abdominal and leg stability. It can be made more difficult be adding this step before lowering your leg: swing your left leg out to the side, still holding your toes. Breathe steadily, and hold for about 5 seconds.

Step 1 Stand with your right hand on your hip and your weight shifted to the right foot.

Step 2 Raise your left knee toward your chest, and take hold of your left foot with your left hand.

Step 3 Extend the left leg out in front of you, keeping hold of the toes with your fingers. Maintain the position for 10 seconds, and then lower the leg. Perform five repetitions per leg.

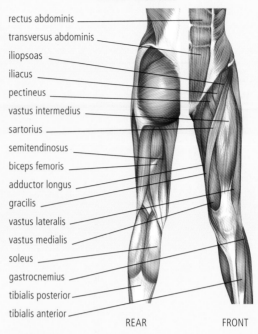

TARGET MUSCLES

- rectus abdominis
- transversus abdominis
- iliopsoas
- iliacus
- pectineus
- vastus intermedius
- sartorius
- semitendinosus
- biceps femoris
- adductor longus
- gracilis
- vastus lateralis
- vastus medialis
- soleus
- gastrocnemius
- tibialis posterior
- tibialis anterior

REAR   FRONT

LEGS

CORRECT ACTION
- Keep your hips straight on and squared up

AVOID
- Bouncing around on the foot

2

3

Kneeling Side Lift

Tone the outer thigh and core with this Pilates exercise. Take care not to let the extended foot touch the floor until the exercise is complete. The Kneeling Side Lift can be made less challenging by propping up your torso on one arm.

WARNING Not advisable if you have wrist pain, shoulder issues, or lower-back pain.

Step 1 Begin by kneeling on the floor, with your right leg outstretched to the side and the left leg lined up under the hips. Place both hands behind your head, with your elbows extended out to the sides.

Step 2 Lift your right leg up off the floor, bringing it as high as your hips. Repeat sequence five to six times. Switch sides, and repeat the sequence with your left leg.

CORRECT ACTION
• Your torso remains aligned to better balance the movement of your leg
• Your neck is relaxed and lengthened
• Your leg is elongated as much as possible

AVOID
• Sinking into your neck or shoulders

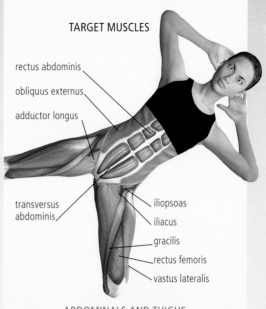

TARGET MUSCLES

rectus abdominis
obliquus externus
adductor longus
transversus abdominis
iliopsoas
iliacus
gracilis
rectus femoris
vastus lateralis

ABDOMINALS AND THIGHS

Lateral Low Lunge

The Lateral Low Lunge enhances the mobility of your hips, and helps loosen the muscles of your glutes and groin. It requires balance, strength, and coordination. Be sure to have properly stretched your thigh muscles before attempting this exercise.

WARNING Not advisable if you have wrist pain, shoulder issues, or lower-back pain.

Step 1 Stand upright with your hips and arms outstretched in front of you, parallel to the floor.

Step 2 Step out to the left. Squat down on your right leg, bending at your hips, while maintaining a neutral spine. Begin to extend your left leg, keeping both feet flat on the floor.

Step 3 Bend your right knee until your thigh is parallel to the floor, and your left leg is fully extended.

Step 4 Keeping your arms parallel to the ground, squeeze your buttocks and press off your right leg to return to the starting position, and repeat. Repeat sequence 10 times on each side.

TARGET MUSCLES

transversus abdominis

adductor longus

adductor magnus

vastus lateralis

sartorius

rectus femoris

THIGHS AND HIPS

CORRECT ACTION
• Your spine remains neutral as you bend your hips
• Your shoulders and neck remain relaxed
• Your knee aligns with the toe of your bent leg
• The gluteal muscles are tight as you bend

AVOID
• Craning your neck as you perform the movement
• Lifting your feet off the floor
• Arching or extending your back

High Lunge

This exercise takes your body into a huge lunge, working the muscles of your lower body as well as the lower portion of your abdomen. The High Lunge helps stretch and strengthen the thighs, particularly the hip flexors; it opens up the groin region, tones the calves, and strengthens your lower back.

WARNING Not advisable if you have wrist pain, shoulder issues, or lower-back pain.

Step 1 Standing tall, move your right foot forward and bend at the hips, bringing your hands down to either side of your foot.

Step 2 Step back with the left foot, keeping your legs in line with your hips. Keep the ball of your right foot in contact with the floor.

Step 3 Press the ball of your right foot on the floor, contract your thigh muscles, and press up to maintain your left leg in a straight position. Hold for five to six seconds.

Step 4 Slowly return to standing position, and then repeat on the right side. Repeat 10 times on each side.

TARGET MUSCLES

- adductor magnus
- gluteus medius
- gluteus maximus
- rectus femoris
- semimembranosus
- vastus lateralis

GLUTES AND THIGHS

CORRECT ACTION
- Your spine is lengthened by maintaining the proper position of your shoulders and upper body

AVOID
- Dropping your back-extended knee to the floor

Towel Fly

The Towel Fly is a great way to give your chest workout a boost by making the most of your body weight. This exercise also recruits numerous other muscles of the arms, back, hips, and abdomen to keep yourself stabilized—master the Towel Fly and you'll see real improvement in your chest, arm, and core strength.

WARNING Not advisable if you have wrist pain, shoulder issues, or lower-back pain.

Step 1 Place a towel on the floor in front of you. Assume the plank position, with your elbows fully extended, and the towel under your hands.

Step 2 Maintaining a rigid plank position and putting your weight into your heels, move your hands together. The towel should bunch together below your sternum.

Step 3 Straighten out the towel by pressing outward with your arms, returning to the starting position. Repeat 10 times.

TARGET MUSCLES

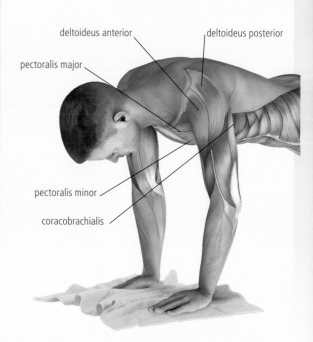

- deltoideus anterior
- deltoideus posterior
- pectoralis major
- pectoralis minor
- coracobrachialis

CHEST AND ARMS

CORRECT ACTION
- Your hands remain aligned directly below your shoulders
- Your weight is distributed evenly between your heels

AVOID
- Allowing your hips to sag
- Lowering your head as you open and close your hands
- Bending your elbows

Body Saw

The Body Saw is practically a combination of a Plank and a Roll-Down, and is a challenging exercise that improves core strength and definition. Planks are tough enough, but they can work your core even harder with just a touch of movement. The Body Saw is a really effective way to work your abdominals without doing hundreds of crunches. It can be made more difficult by elevating your legs on a step, Bosu ball, or Swiss ball.

Step 1 Begin by kneeling on the floor, streching out and resting on your forearms with your palms flat on the floor.

Step 2 Lift yourself up so that you are balanced on your forearms and toes.

Step 3 Rock your body forward and then backward for three sets of 10 repetitions (working up to 20).

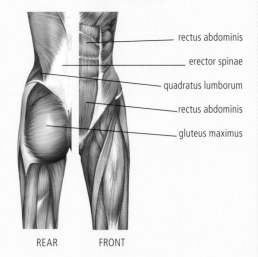

TARGET MUSCLES

rectus abdominis
erector spinae
quadratus lumborum
rectus abdominis
gluteus maximus

REAR FRONT

ABDOMINALS AND GLUTES

CORRECT ACTION
• Keep your body fully extended and in one straight line

AVOID
• Overusing your lower back by rising higher than parallel to the ground

Swimming

The Swimming exercise improves lower-back strength and support. The difficulty of this exercise can be increased by raising both arms and legs at the same time (commonly known as the Superman).

Step 1 Lie on your stomach with your arms stretched out in front of you and your legs stretched out behind.

Step 2 Raise your left arm and right leg off the floor at the same time, along with your head and shoulders, then lower them all back down.

Step 3 Repeat the exercise with your opposite limbs.

Step 4 Complete 10 repetitions per side.

CORRECT ACTION
• Raise your arms and legs as high as possible

AVOID
• Overstressing the neck

TARGET MUSCLES

latissimus dorsi

rectus abdominis

erector spinae

obliquus externus

hip flexors

gluteus maximus

biceps femoris

LOWER BACK   REAR   FRONT

MODIFICATION

This exercise can be made more difficult by raising both arms and legs at the same time—this is known as the Superman.

Hip Twist

Hip Twists are a great toning exercise that will help tone your waist and strengthen your core. This exercise strengthens the oblique muscles, helping to create a more defined waist and better supported back. The Hip Twist also works your shoulders and abs at the same time.

WARNING Not advisable if you have wrist pain, shoulder issues, or lower-back pain.

Step 1 Begin by sitting on the floor with your arms behind your body, supporting your weight. Your legs should be parallel and raised to a high diagonal.

Step 2 Engage your abdominals and shoulders for stabilization.

Step 3 Bring both legs across the body to the right.

Step 4 Continue to circle your legs across your body and down as low as pelvic stabilization can be maintained.

Step 5 Return your legs to the starting position. Repeat two to six times in each direction.

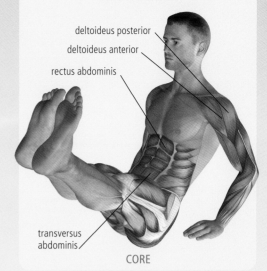

TARGET MUSCLES

- deltoideus posterior
- deltoideus anterior
- rectus abdominis
- transversus abdominis

CORE

CORRECT ACTION
- Your legs are lengthened as you move from side to side
- Your arms push out of your shoulders to better engage your torso
- Your neck is elongated

AVOID
- Tensing your neck and shoulder muscles

Russian Twist

The Russian Twist is an exercise that is used to work the abdomen muscles by performing a twisting motion on the abdomen. The exercise is used to build explosiveness in the upper torso, which can help in sports such as baseball and golf.

WARNING Not advisable if you have shoulder issues or lower-back pain.

Step 1 Sit with your knees bent and your feet flat on the floor. Lift up through your torso. Raise your arms parallel to the floor so that your hands are outstretched above your knees.

Step 2 Rotate your upper body to the right, reaching toward the floor with your hands.

Step 3 Pass back through the center and rotate to the left. Repeat 10 times on each side.

CORRECT ACTION
• Your feet remain planted on the floor as you twist
• Your knees are squeezed together
• Your neck and shoulders remain relaxed

AVOID
• Shifting your feet or knees to the side as you twist

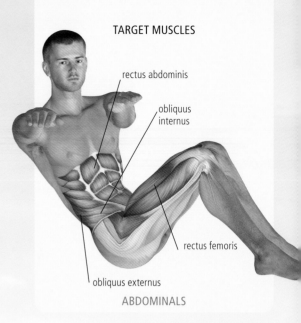

TARGET MUSCLES

rectus abdominis

obliquus internus

rectus femoris

obliquus externus

ABDOMINALS

MODIFICATION

More difficult: Lift your feet off the floor and rotate your torso from side to side, pulling your knees in and out as you twist.

Twist

Your obliques—located on the sides of the torso—are responsible for bending and rotating your torso and are used in almost every activity. To work them properly, incorporate moves such as the Twist.

WARNING Not advisable if you have wrist pain, shoulder issues, or lower-back pain.

Step 1 Start on your right side with your legs outstretched and pressed firmly together. Press your right hip into the floor, and use both hands to support your torso.

Step 2 Position your right hand directly beneath your shoulder and press your body up into a side plank with side-arm balance.

Step 3 Drawing your navel into your spine, extend your left arm toward the ceiling.

Step 4 Bring your left arm down and across your torso, rotating the upper body to the right. Hold for a count of ten.

Step 5 Return to the starting position, with your hip on the floor and both hands supporting your torso. Repeat the sequence four to six times, and then switch sides.

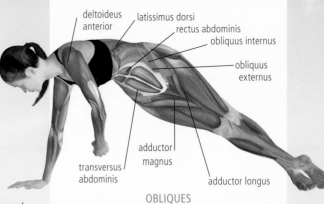

TARGET MUSCLES

deltoideus anterior
latissimus dorsi
rectus abdominis
obliquus internus
obliquus externus
transversus abdominis
adductor magnus
adductor longus

OBLIQUES

CORRECT ACTION
- Your limbs are elongated as much as possible
- Your shoulders remain stable
- Your hips are lifted up high to reduce the weight on your upper body

AVOID
- Allowing your shoulder to sink into its socket

Free Weight Exercises

Free weights have the unique ability to harness multiple muscles together, resulting in increased strength and power throughout the body. Free weights such as kettlebells and dumbbells require precision, timing, and to some degree, momentum to accomplish challenging movements. There is also the advantage that free weight exercises can all be done at home, circumventing the need for a gym membership.

Kettlebell Figure-Eight

The Kettlebell Figure-Eight is a strength builder, primarily of the trunk and hips, but it challenges your whole body. Strength, coordination, timing, and accuracy are required to perform this exercise correctly. The Kettlebell Figure-Eight is slow-paced and is performed for longer amounts of time than most exercises—in doing so it helps to develop your "slow strength" and muscular endurance rather than explosive power or speed.

Step 1 Begin with a kettlebell in hand, legs in a wide stance with your glutes out, bent over and with a flat back.

Step 2 Start by passing the kettlebell from one hand to another between the legs.

Step 3 Reach from behind the leg with the receiving hand and switch the kettlebell.

CORRECT ACTION
- Look for slow and controlled repetitions
- Keep your back flat throughout the movement
- Move your hips side to side during the movement

AVOID
- Excessive speed
- Bouncy repetitions
- Shallow or incomplete passes

Step 4 Make 20 passes between the hands, in and out of your legs.

Step 5 After completing 20 passes, switch directions. Instead of switching hands, swing the kettlebell back out with the same hand and back in front of the same leg it just circled around.

Step 6 Perform another 20 passes.

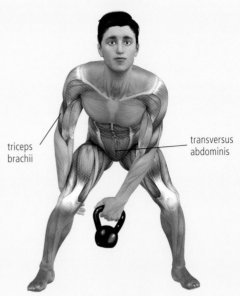

TARGET MUSCLES

triceps brachii

transversus abdominis

TRUNK AND HIPS

3

Turkish Get-Up

The Turkish Get-Up is a highly functional movement that requires all the muscles of the body working together in order to perform the exercise properly. It produces great stability in the hips and balance throughout the body. Its center of focus is the core from which all movement begins.

WARNING Not advisable if you have wrist pain, shoulder issues, or lower-back pain.

CORRECT ACTION
- A tight core throughout
- Keep your eyes on the dumbbell
- Take your time

AVOID
- Excessive speed
- Not shifting your hips
- Not using your core

Step 1 Begin on your back on the ground with one arm raised straight out above your chest holding a dumbbell or kettlebell, and the other at your side.

Step 2 Flex the same sided knee with that foot flat on the floor while supporting your weight on the opposite elbow.

Step 3 Tuck the opposite leg underneath your body.

Step 4 Rise up with the same outstretched arm over your head.

Step 5 Return to the start and perform 10 repetitions per side.

TARGET MUSCLES

trapezius

triceps brachii

rectus abdominis

erector spinae

vastus intermedeus

REAR   FRONT

CORE

3

4

Wheel Rollout

An important role of your midsection is stabilization. This exercise tests your ability to maintain muscular tension through the midsection while maintaining correct form. Once you become accomplished at this suprisingly challenging exercise, you can perform it moving the ab roller to the sides in a diagonal fashion as opposed to straight forward. This version places more emphasis on the obliques. You can also place a barbell plate on your back to add to the difficulty.

WARNING Not advisable if you have wrist pain, shoulder issues, or lower-back pain.

Step 1 Start by kneeling on the floor, gripping the handles of an ab roller with both hands.

Step 2 Slowly roll the wheel out, keeping your back straight.

Step 3 Roll out as far as you can, maintaining control—ideally until you are completely straight.

Step 4 Pull the wheel back, tensing your abdominals, until you are back to the start position.

Step 5 Repeat until failure.

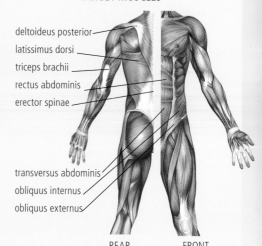

TARGET MUSCLES

deltoideus posterior
latissimus dorsi
triceps brachii
rectus abdominis
erector spinae

transversus abdominis
obliquus internus
obliquus externus

REAR   FRONT

CORE

CORRECT ACTION
• Keep your head down
• Tuck your chin in as you roll out
• Keep your spine straight

AVOID
• Arching your back

Dumbbell Sit-Up

Sit-Ups train your core muscles to help you achieve better flexibility and balance, and to improve overall body strength. They help build the muscles in your abdominals, lower back, and hip flexors. Adding dumbbells increases the intensity level of the move, creating weight resistance and adding an arm-workout element. You can increase the weight of the dumbbells as you become proficient in the exercise.

WARNING Not advisable if you have lower-back pain.

Step 1 Start by lying on the floor with your knees slightly bent, holding a dumbbell in each hand.

Step 2 Contract your abdominals as you raise your torso into a sit-up position, keeping the dumbbells at shoulder level.

Step 3 Lower yourself slowly back to the floor—the slower the movement, the more effective the exercise.

Step 4 Repeat until failure.

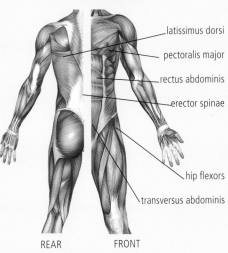

TARGET MUSCLES

- latissimus dorsi
- pectoralis major
- rectus abdominis
- erector spinae
- hip flexors
- transversus abdominis

REAR   FRONT

CORE

CORRECT ACTION
- A smooth range of motion
- Keep the dumbbells at shoulder level
- Slow movement

AVOID
- Stressing your lower back

Kettlebell Double Clean

You should learn how to clean with a set of very light kettlebells. Keep your arms loose with just enough tension to perform the exercise. However, your body should be locked tight and braced. Using a lighter pair of kettlebells will allow you to put all your focus on the swing and redirection, rather than on just getting the kettlebells into place. You can also add a press to the movement, raising the kettlebells above your head at the end of the motion.

WARNING Not advisable if you have wrist pain or shoulder issues.

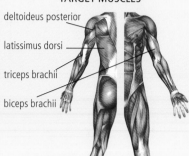

TARGET MUSCLES

deltoideus posterior

latissimus dorsi

triceps brachii

biceps brachii

REAR   FRONT

UPPER ARMS

Step 1 Start in a squat position, with a kettlebell in each hand. The midpoint of the handles should be aligned with the midpoint of your feet.

Step 2 Internally rotate the arms as you reach down so that when you hold the handles your thumbs are pointing back behind your legs.

Step 3 Tense your abdominals, drive your feet into the floor, and thrust your hips forward to create the momentum required to clean the kettlebells up into the rack position.

Step 4 Once the kettlebells are in motion, loosen your grip to allow the kettlebell to wrap around your forearm as it slides into position.

Step 5 Repeat 15 times.

CORRECT ACTION
• Keep your eyes forward to help keep your body squared and back straight
• Your neck is elongated
• Use tight, controlled exhalation

AVOID
• Letting the kettlebells hit your forearms

Stiff-Leg Dead Lift

This exercise can be performed with either dumbbells or a barbell. It needs to be treated with the utmost respect: pay special attention to make sure you do not round your back as you move the torso down; the back must always be straight. A jerking action—or using too much weight—can injure your back.

WARNING Not advisable if you have lower-back pain.

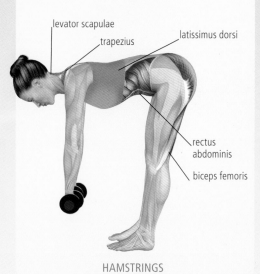

TARGET MUSCLES

levator scapulae

trapezius

latissimus dorsi

rectus abdominis

biceps femoris

HAMSTRINGS

Step 1 Holding a pair of dumbbells loosely against your outer thighs, stand with your feet shoulder-width apart, your knees slightly bent, and your rear pushed out slightly.

Step 2 Maintaining a flat back at all times, bring the dumbbells around in front of you and lower them toward the floor, feeling the main stretch in the back of the legs.

Step 3 Return to the starting position and complete three sets of 15 repetitions.

CORRECT ACTION
• Keep your back flat at all times

AVOID
• Straining your lower back excessively

Seated Barbell Twist

Breathing is very important to this exercise: exhale as you twist your upper body to one side, allowing the barbell to follow. Stop when you feel your oblique muscles stretching. Inhale as you return your upper body to the starting position in a slow, controlled manner. The version shown here is the easiest version; it can, of course, be made more difficult by adding weights to the barbell.

WARNING Not advisable if you have lower-back pain.

Step 1 Start by sitting on a flat bench, with a barbell placed on your shoulders.

Step 2 Grip the bar with your palms facing forward and make sure your hands are wider than shoulder-width apart.

Step 3 While keeping your feet and head still, move your waist from side to side so that your oblique muscles feel a contraction.

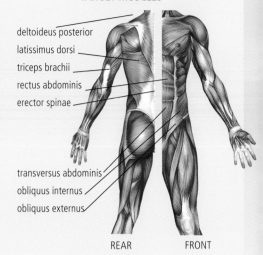

TARGET MUSCLES

deltoideus posterior
latissimus dorsi
triceps brachii
rectus abdominis
erector spinae

transversus abdominis
obliquus internus
obliquus externus

REAR   FRONT

ABDOMINALS AND OBLIQUES

CORRECT ACTION
- Breathe out while you twist
- Keep your head straight and your feet still

AVOID
- Twisting more than your waist will allow

Standing Plate Twist

Use a barbell plate and rotate side to side to fire your core muscles. When you perform this motion standing, it becomes a functional exercise, which tends to burn more fat and allows everyday activities to become simpler.

WARNING Not advisable if you have wrist pain or lower-back pain.

Step 1 Start by standing in an upright position.

Step 2 Hold a weighted plate in front of your chest, with your arms slightly bent.

Step 3 Keep your feet still and rotate your torso from the waist.

Step 4 Swivel your torso back all the way around to the other side.

Step 5 Repeat 30 times.

CORRECT ACTION
• Compress your abdomen
• Keep your back straight

AVOID
• Twisting more than your waist will allow

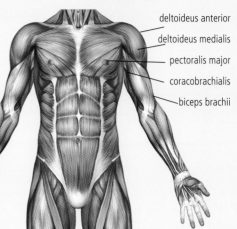

TARGET MUSCLES

deltoideus anterior
deltoideus medialis
pectoralis major
coracobrachialis
biceps brachii

SHOULDERS

Seated Dumbbell Press

The Seated Dumbbell Press is one of the most popular muscle builders for the shoulders. It can be performed on an adjustable-angle bench with the back set to 90 degrees. But for added difficulty, and also to work your abs, sit on a Swiss ball instead.

WARNING Not advisable if you have lower-back pain.

TARGET MUSCLES

deltoideus anterior

trapezius

triceps brachii

latissimus dorsi

rectus abdominus

erector spinae

REAR   FRONT

SHOULDERS

Step 1 Sit on a Swiss ball, holding a dumbbell in each hand at shoulder height.

Step 2 Keeping your eyes facing forward, slowly raise the dumbbell in your left hand above your head until your arm is almost fully extended.

Step 3 Do not pause at the top of the movement, and immediately begin lowering the dumbbell back down to the starting position.

Step 4 Repeat this movement immediately with your right arm.

Step 5 Repeat 30 times.

CORRECT ACTION
- Use the longest range of motion possible
- Control the dumbbells throughout the movement

AVOID
- Adding too much weight too soon

Kettlebell Squat

With this exercise it is important to remember that if you do not squat deep enough (thighs parallel with the floor), then you are not engaging your glutes properly. Shallow squatting will only work your quads (thigh muscles) and not the largest muscles in the body.

WARNING Not advisable if you have lower-back pain.

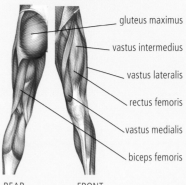

TARGET MUSCLES

gluteus maximus
vastus intermedius
vastus lateralis
rectus femoris
vastus medialis
biceps femoris

REAR   FRONT

THIGHS AND GLUTES

Step 1 Stand upright, holding a kettlebell in each hand.

Step 2 Start the movement by pushing the hips backward.

Step 3 Squat down until your thighs are parallel with the floor.

Step 4 Push the floor away from you on your way up.

Step 5 Repeat 15 times.

CORRECT ACTION
• Keep the weight on your heels and outside of the feet
• Your neck is elongated
• Your thighs should be at least parallel with the floor
• Breathe in as you descend, breathe out as you ascend

AVOID
• Bending your back

Cable and Band Exercises

Cable exercises offer unique angles and resistance throughout to make them a welcome addition to one's exercise routine. Traditionally thought of as "finisher" exercises, when done properly, cables offer maximal tension on muscles to enable them to grow back stronger and more flexible with more range.

Standing Cable Lift

The Standing Cable Lift is a great exercise for the obliques, abdominals, forearms, and triceps. It can also be performed with a medicine ball. You could use a double-handed rope extension to ensure that both hands are pulling equally.

WARNING Avoid this exercise if you have lower-back pain, wrist pain, or shoulder issues.

Step 1 Start off by connecting a cable to the lowest setting on a cable machine. Grab the cable with both hands and stand to the side of the machine with your feet shoulder-width apart.

Step 2 Slowly pull the handle up across your body, twisting your torso and extending through your hips, until your arms are fully extended and your hands are higher than your head.

Step 3 Hold this position for a count of three, squeezing your abs, then slowly release back to the starting position.

Step 4 Repeat for as many reps and sets as desired.

CORRECT ACTION
- Slow movement through the exercise
- Keep your feet planted on the floor
- A full range of motion

AVOID
- A haphazard pattern
- Engaging your lower back
- Excessive speed

TARGET MUSCLES

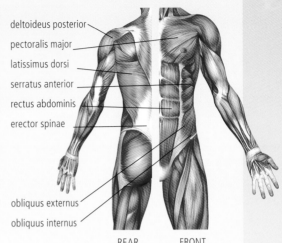

deltoideus posterior
pectoralis major
latissimus dorsi
serratus anterior
rectus abdominis
erector spinae

obliquus externus
obliquus internus

REAR   FRONT

OBLIQUES, ABDOMINALS, AND LOWER BACK

Kneeling Cable Crunch

The Kneeling Cable Crunch takes the standard crunch and adds resistance to it, thereby making this a very effective core-strengthening exercise suitable for all levels.

WARNING Avoid this exercise if you have lower-back pain.

Step 1 Begin on your knees, with a rope held around your neck, facing away from a weight stack, set to a moderate resistance.

Step 2 Bend forward at the waist, keeping your neck tucked, and crunch downward, until your elbows are resting on your thighs.

Step 3 Contract the abdominals, then return to the starting position, and repeat for 30 repetitions.

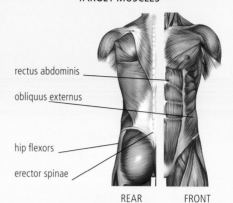

TARGET MUSCLES

rectus abdominis

obliquus externus

hip flexors

erector spinae

REAR   FRONT

ABDOMINALS

CORRECT ACTION
- Maintain a full range of motion
- Contract the muscles together at the bottom of the movement
- A straightened torso at the top

AVOID
- Excessive speed
- A shortened range of motion
- Using too much neck at the expense of your abdominals

Standing Cable Crunch

The Standing Cable Crunch is as effective as the kneeling version and offers a good variant on this superb core-strengthening movement. The standing movement offers just as much tension and range as the kneeling, but with added dimension.

Step 1 Begin in a standing position, with a rope held around your neck, facing away from a weight stack, set to a moderate resistance with your elbows pointing toward the ground.

Step 2 Bend forward at the waist, keeping your neck tucked, and crunch downward, until your elbows are nearly resting on your upper thighs.

Step 3 Contract the abdominals, then return to the starting position, and repeat for 30 repetitions.

CORRECT ACTION
- Maintain a full range of motion
- Contract the muscles together at the bottom of the movement
- Your knees should be slightly bent

AVOID
- Excessive speed
- A shortened range of motion
- Using too much neck at the expense of your abdominals

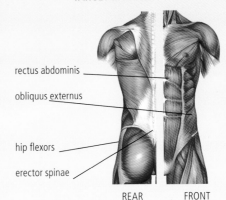

TARGET MUSCLES

rectus abdominis

obliquus externus

hip flexors

erector spinae

REAR   FRONT

OBLIQUES AND ABDOMINALS

Cable Rotations

One of the keys with this exercise is to use a weight that's comfortable and not too strenuous—you should be able to do 15 repetitions comfortably. You need to focus on form with this exercise—when you pull the cable across, try to squeeze out the motion in your obliques. Plant your feet and rotate only your upper body. To modify the exercise, pull from high to low—this is called a Woodchopper.

Step 1 Stand holding a cable close to the abdomen. The cable should extend to the side.

Step 2 Tighten your abdominals and slowly turn your upper body away from the cable anchor.

Step 3 Hold briefly before returning to the starting position. After one set of 15 repetitions, face the opposite direction and repeat.

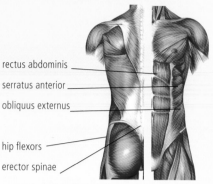

TARGET MUSCLES

rectus abdominis

serratus anterior

obliquus externus

hip flexors

erector spinae

REAR   FRONT

OBLIQUES AND ABDOMINALS

CORRECT ACTION
• Keep your feet still
• Rotate your whole torso
• Pull and release the cable slowly

AVOID
• Moving your feet
• Rotating too far at the hips
• Excessive speed

Triceps Overhead Extension with Bands

This exercise can be performed standing or sitting on a bench (with or without back support). You can also use a dumbbell or weighted plate instead of bands or cable.

WARNING Not advisable if you have shoulder or back issues.

Step 1 Grip the bands with both hands using a neutral grip.

Step 2 Fully extend your arms until your hands are directly above your head, pointing to the ceiling.

Step 3 Slowly lower the rope behind your head, keeping your upper arms as still as possible, inhaling as you do so.

Step 4 When your triceps are fully extended, hold for a count of three while squeezing your triceps.

Step 5 Return to the starting position by flexing your triceps and extending your arms, exhaling as you do so.

CORRECT ACTION
• Keep your elbows close to your head
• Keep your upper arms motionless

AVOID
• Engaging your lower back
• Excessive speed

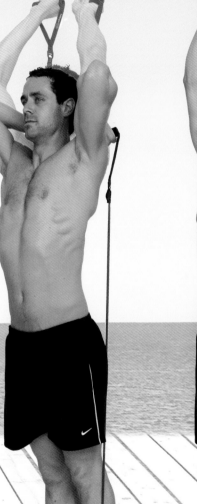

TARGET MUSCLES

pectoralis major
trapezius
triceps brachii
rectus abdominis
erector spinae

REAR   FRONT

TRICEPS AND UPPER BACK

Bosu Ball Exercises

The Bosu ball has the unique advantage of providing two working surfaces, making it doubly effective and increasing the amount of exercises that can be performed on it. Its core strengthening, balancing, and stabilization benefits make it a fun must-have in your workouts.

Bosu Ball Crunch

The inclusion of a Bosu ball while performing crunches results in more direct tension on the abdominal muscles as well as a pronounced effect on core strength. The Bosu Ball Crunch leverages the fully stretched position and the resultant reflex for a stronger contraction than a floor crunch. If a Bosu ball is not available, use a small Swiss ball (45–55 centimeters in diameter) or some firm cushions.

Step 1 Lie on your back on the dome part of a Bosu ball, with your legs slightly bent and your palms placed on your ears and your elbows flared outward.

Step 2 With your head and neck just hanging off the ball and tension present in the abdominals, raise your head and shoulders off the ground while contracting your trunk toward your waist.

Step 3 Lower your torso back to the starting position and repeat for up to 30 repetitions.

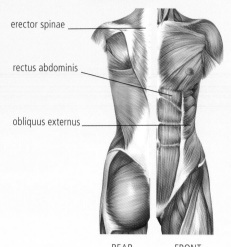

TARGET MUSCLES

erector spinae

rectus abdominis

obliquus externus

REAR   FRONT

ABDOMINALS AND OBLIQUES

CORRECT ACTION
• Maintain a precise range of motion
• Tension on the abdominals

AVOID
• Using the neck
• Bouncy and speedy repetitions

Bosu Ball Sit-Up

The Bosu Ball Sit-Up is a short axis-specific abdominal exercise that improves core control. This exercise is designed to improve control through a large range of motion. The exercise can be made more difficult by holding a dumbbell or weight behind your head.

Step 1 Lie down on your back on the dome part of a Bosu ball, with your legs slightly bent and your palms placed on your ears and your elbows flared outward.

Step 2 With your head and neck just hanging off the ball and tension present in the abdominals, raise your head and shoulders off the ground while contracting your trunk toward your waist.

Step 3 Keep moving up until you are sitting in an upright position.

Step 4 Lower your torso back to the starting position and repeat for up to 30 repetitions.

CORRECT ACTION
- Maintain a precise range of motion
- Tension on the abdominals

AVOID
- Using the neck
- Bouncy and speedy repetitions

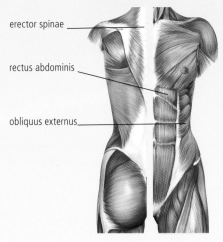

TARGET MUSCLES

erector spinae

rectus abdominis

obliquus externus

REAR   FRONT

ABDOMINALS AND OBLIQUES

Bosu Ball Bicycle Crunches

Bosu Ball Bicycle Crunches are an advanced version of the regular Bosu Ball Crunch that effectively calls both the upper-body and lower-body muscles into play. It is a challenging exercise upon which core strength is built.

Step 1 Lie down on your back on the dome part of a Bosu ball, your legs bent and your palms placed behind your ears with your elbows flared outward.

Step 2 With your head and neck just hanging off the ball and tension present in the abdominals, raise your head and shoulders off the ground while contracting your trunk toward your waist.

Step 3 Rotate your elbow toward its opposite knee, which you lift toward your chest at the same time.

Step 4 Lower and repeat with the other leg and its opposing side for 15 repetitions per side.

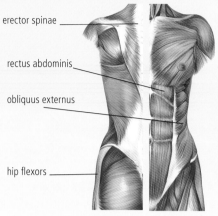

TARGET MUSCLES

erector spinae

rectus abdominis

obliquus externus

hip flexors

REAR   FRONT

ABDOMINALS AND OBLIQUES

CORRECT ACTION
• Lead from your belly button
• A controlled lowering
• A precise and sharp rotation

AVOID
• Overusing your neck
• Stressing your lower back
• Pulling your head too far forward

Bosu Ball Leg Scissors

Bosu Ball Leg Scissors are highly effective for the abdominals, especially the section below the navel. The Leg Scissors is an extremely challenging exercise, as you change your leg position in midair. The addition of doing it on a Bosu ball makes it even harder by adding a balance challenge. You'll need to use additional leg strength in order to push off against the ball, and to engage your abs and lats to control your movement. Aim for minimal wobbling.

Step 1 Lie with the center of your back on top of the Bosu ball.

Step 2 Lean back slightly while maintaining a flat back and keeping your core tight. Raise your legs slightly off the ground.

Step 3 Alternately raise one leg up and down, followed by the other, 20 times.

Step 4 Now open and close your legs in an overlapping scissorslike motion for 20 repetitions.

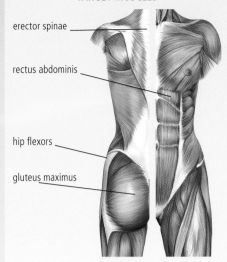

TARGET MUSCLES

erector spinae

rectus abdominis

hip flexors

gluteus maximus

REAR   FRONT

LEGS AND ABDOMINALS

CORRECT ACTION
- Keep your abs drawn in tightly
- Keep your legs slightly bent throughout
- A precise and sharp range of motion

AVOID
- Overbending the knees
- Stressing your lower back

Bosu Ball Side Plank

The Bosu Ball Side Plank takes the already effective side plank movement and makes it even more challenging and effective by adding the unstable dome surface. There are three feet positions you can use with the side plank, of varying degrees of difficulty. For the easiest position, bend your bottom leg by 90 degrees so your knee is taking some of the weight off your top leg and core; the regular pose has one foot in front of the other; the advanced pose calls for the top foot to be directly on top of the bottom foot, as shown here.

Step 1 Lie on your side with your torso on the dome part of the Bosu ball, with your legs straight and parallel to one another.

Step 2 Bend your arm to a 90-degree angle with your knuckles facing forward. Bend your other arm, resting the hand on your hip.

Step 3 Push off your forearm while raising your hips off the ground until your body forms a straight line.

Step 4 Perform 15 repetitions, then repeat on the other side.

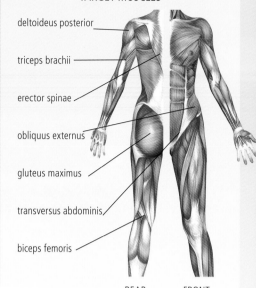

TARGET MUSCLES

- deltoideus posterior
- triceps brachii
- erector spinae
- obliquus externus
- gluteus maximus
- transversus abdominis
- biceps femoris

REAR   FRONT

ABDOMINALS AND OBLIQUES

CORRECT ACTION
- Breathe throughout the exercise
- Keep your abdominals contracted

AVOID
- Leaning your shoulder back too far in the contracted position
- Holding your breath
- Using too much of your shoulders and upper back

Bosu Ball Seated Leg Tucks

Bosu Ball Seated Leg Tucks are an effective core strengthener for the lower abdominal area. They require balance, precision, and stability. You can also perform this exercise on a mat on the floor just by placing your arms to the sides. In this case, the legs will be stretched and elevated slightly over the floor. Also, as you become more advanced, you can hold a dumbbell in between your feet.

WARNING Be very careful when adding weight to this exercise, as if you add too much it could result in a hernia.

TARGET MUSCLES

rectus abdominis

erector spinae

hip flexors

gluteus maximus

REAR   FRONT

ABDOMINALS

Step 1 Sit on the dome of a Bosu ball with your feet on the ground and your hands on the side of the dome.

Step 2 Start by raising both legs off the ground so that your legs form a V shape with your torso.

Step 3 Bring your legs close toward your chest while bending your knees.

Step 4 Lower and perform 20 repetitions.

CORRECT ACTION
- A controlled range of motion
- Proper sync and tempo

AVOID
- Stressing the lower back
- Excessively using your neck
- Pushing your upper body too far forward

Foam Roller Exercises

It may not look like much, but a foam roller is one of the most valuable, inexpensive, and versatile pieces of exercise equipment out there. It is a great strength-training tool, helping to engage key muscles you want to tone, like your arms, abs, thighs, and glutes, and because the foam roller is an unstable surface, it can replace a Bosu ball or Swiss ball in many exercises, helping to improve your balance and fire up your core muscles.

Quadruped Knee Pull-In

The Quadruped Knee Pull-In targets your abdominals, thighs, and triceps, and helps improve core stability. Focus on a slow, controlled movement to get maximum benefit from the exercise. It can be made more difficult by bending your arms as you roll in, creating more instability.

WARNING Not advisable if you have shoulder pain, wrist pain, or knee issues.

Step 1 Place the foam roller on the floor. Kneel on the roller, with your hands placed on the floor in front of you. Your hands should be slightly in front of your torso, and your hips should be lifted off your heels.

Step 2 Round out your torso as you pull your knees toward your hands, allowing the roller to move toward your feet. Repeat 15 times for two sets.

CORRECT ACTION
- Round your back as you draw your knees inward
- Relax your head
- Smooth transitions

AVOID
- Allowing your shoulders to lift toward your ears
- Moving your head forward

TARGET MUSCLES

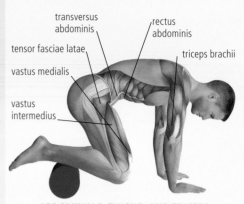

transversus abdominis
rectus abdominis
tensor fasciae latae
triceps brachii
vastus medialis
vastus intermedius

ABDOMINALS, THIGHS, AND TRICEPS

MODIFICATION

More difficult: Follow previous instructions, and then bend your elbows into a push-up, straighten, and roll slowly to the starting position.

Hamstring Roll

As its name suggests, the Hamstring Roll is a great workout for your hamstrings, but you'll also feel a burn in your triceps and abs. Only roll as far as feels comfortable, as the roll-back is more challenging than the roll-out.

WARNING Avoid this exercise if you have lower-back or shoulder issues.

Step 1 Sit on the floor with your legs outstretched in front of you, with the foam roller placed under your knees. Place your hands on the floor to support your torso, your fingers pointing toward your buttocks.

Step 2 Press into the floor to raise your hips, keeping your legs firm.

Step 3 Draw your hips backward through your arms, rolling your legs over the roller. Drop your head so that your gaze is directed at your thighs.

Step 4 Roll on the roller back to the starting position, keeping your hips lifted off the floor. Repeat 15 times.

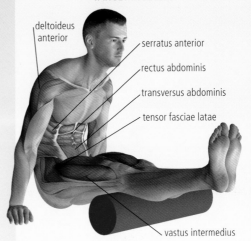

TARGET MUSCLES

deltoideus anterior

serratus anterior

rectus abdominis

transversus abdominis

tensor fasciae latae

vastus intermedius

HAMSTRINGS AND TRICEPS

CORRECT ACTION
- All movement happens at the same time
- Your neck and shoulders remain relaxed throughout the exercise

AVOID
- Allowing your shoulders to lift toward your ears
- Bending your knees as you pull back

Single-Leg Calf Press

The Single-Leg Calf Press is a multifunctional exercise that helps to improve core, pelvic, and shoulder stability. It is a great workout for your shoulders, abdominals, hamstrings, and triceps. If you find the exercise too challenging, don't raise off the floor.

WARNING Not advisable if you have shoulder pain or wrist pain.

Step 1 Sit on the floor with your legs outstretched in front of you, with the foam roller placed under your knees. Place your hands on the floor to support your torso, your fingers pointing toward your buttocks.

Step 2 Press into the floor to lift your hips, keeping your legs firm.

Step 3 Lift one leg off the roller and hold it steady, making sure not to drop your hips.

Step 4 Keep the leg lifted, and press your opposite leg into the roller, drawing your hips back toward your hands.

Step 5 Return to the starting position, rolling your calf muscle along the roller and keeping your lifted leg straight in the air. Repeat 15 times on each leg.

TARGET MUSCLES

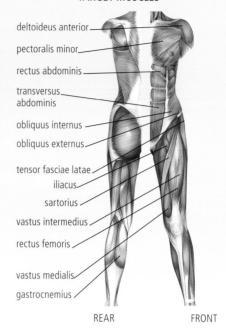

deltoideus anterior
pectoralis minor
rectus abdominis
transversus abdominis
obliquus internus
obliquus externus
tensor fasciae latae
iliacus
sartorius
vastus intermedius
rectus femoris
vastus medialis
gastrocnemius

REAR   FRONT

CORE AND LEGS

CORRECT ACTION
- Your lifted leg forms a long, straight line
- Your hips remain elevated throughout the exercise

AVOID
- Allowing your shoulders to lift toward your ears
- Bending your knees
- Bending your elbows

Roller Triceps Dip

Roller Triceps Dips are a challenging exercise for your triceps. Be sure to have thoroughly stretched your upper arms before attempting it. This exercise also works your abdominals, shoulder stabilizers, and hamstrings, and helps improve core and shoulder stability.

WARNING Not advisable if you have shoulder pain, wrist pain, or knee issues.

Step 1 Sit on the floor with your legs outstretched, the foam roller behind you. Place both hands on the foam roller, with your fingers facing toward your buttocks, elbows bent.

Step 2 Press through your legs and straighten your arms to lift your hips and shoulders.

Step 3 Keeping your shoulders pressed down away from your ears, bend your elbows and dip your trunk up and down. The foam roller should not move. Repeat 15 times for two sets.

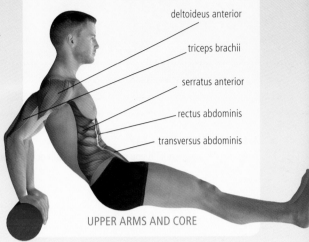

TARGET MUSCLES

deltoideus anterior

triceps brachii

serratus anterior

rectus abdominis

transversus abdominis

UPPER ARMS AND CORE

CORRECT ACTION
- Your legs remain firm, with your knees straight
- Your neck and shoulders remain relaxed throughout the exercise
- The roller remains firmly pressed to the floor

AVOID
- Allowing your shoulders to lift toward your ears
- Shifting the roller as you move up and down

Diagonal Crunch

The Diagonal Crunch targets your triceps, abs, shoulders, and hamstrings. It has the added benefit of helping to improve stability in your core, pelvis, and shoulders.

WARNING This exercise is not advisable if you have back pain or neck pain.

Step 1 Lie lengthwise on the foam roller so that it follows the line of your spine. Your buttocks and upper back should both be in contact with the roller.

Step 2 With your legs straight and your feet pressed firmly into the floor, extend your arms over your head.

Step 3 Raise your head, neck, and shoulders as if to do a crunch. Leave your right leg and left arm down on the ground, using your hand for support. Raise your left leg and right arm, and reach for your ankle.

Step 4 Slowly roll down the roller, dropping your raised arm and leg. Repeat on the opposite leg and arm. Repeat 15 times on each side.

CORRECT ACTION
- Your legs remain firm throughout the exercise
- Your buttocks and shoulders remain in contact with the roller throughout the exercise

AVOID
- Allowing your shoulders to lift toward your ears
- Bending the knees

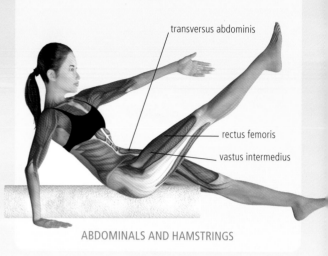

TARGET MUSCLES

transversus abdominis

rectus femoris

vastus intermedius

ABDOMINALS AND HAMSTRINGS

MODIFICATION

More difficult: Keep one leg on the floor for support, and reach both arms toward the raised leg as you crunch up.

Roller Push-Up

The Roller Push-Up helps to improve stability in your core, pelvis, and shoulders. It is a great abdominal exercise, and also targets your chest muscles and shoulder stabilizers.

WARNING This exercise is not advisable if you have lower-back pain, shoulder pain, or neck pain.

Step 1 Kneel on the floor, with the roller placed crosswise in front of you. Place your hands on the roller with your fingers pointed away from you.

Step 2 Press into a plank position, lifting your knees and straightening your legs. Keep your hips level with your shoulders, and without allowing your shoulders to sink, bend your elbows and lower your chest to the roller. Avoid any roller movement throughout the motion.

Step 3 Return to the starting position by pressing upward, straightening your elbows, and maintaining a straight spine. Repeat 15 times for two sets.

TARGET MUSCLES

teres major
teres minor
pectoralis minor
rectus abdominis
pectoralis major
triceps brachii
biceps brachii

CHEST AND ABDOMINALS

CORRECT ACTION
- A single plane of movement, with your body forming a straight line from shoulders to ankle
- Your neck and shoulders remain relaxed throughout the exercise

AVOID
- Allowing your shoulders to lift toward your ears
- Bending your knees
- Raising or lowering your body in segments

Supine Marches

Supine Marches create a great workout for your abdominal muscles, and work to improve core and pelvic stability. Performed regularly, you'll also notice benefits to your quadriceps.

WARNING This exercise is not advisable if you have lower-back pain, shoulder pain, or neck pain.

Step 1 Lie lengthwise on the foam roller so that it follows the line of your spine. Place your arms on the floor by your sides, bending your knees so that your feet rest flat on the floor.

Step 2 Pointing your toes and keeping the hips from lifting or shifting, raise one knee toward your chest.

Step 3 Switch legs, again being careful not to allow your hips to lift.

Step 4 Repeat 15 times on each leg as you establish a smooth "marching" rhythm.

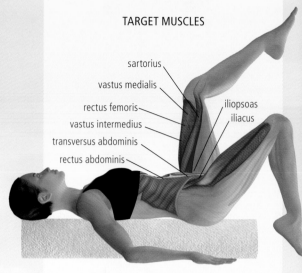

TARGET MUSCLES

sartorius
vastus medialis
rectus femoris
vastus intermedius
transversus abdominis
rectus abdominis
iliopsoas
iliacus

ABDOMINALS AND QUADRICEPS

CORRECT ACTION
- Your legs remain firm and your toes pointed
- Your neck and shoulders remain relaxed throughout the exercise
- Your hands and forearms lie flat on the floor

AVOID
- Allowing your shoulders to lift toward your ears
- Allowing your hips and lower back to lift off the roller during the movement

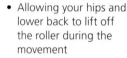

Iliotibial Band Release

This is a challenging exercise that is designed to release the iliotibial band. It may be uncomfortable at first, but will become easier with repetition. It also works your lateral thigh muscles and scapular stabilizers.

WARNING This exercise is not advisable if you have back pain or shoulder pain.

Step 1 Lie on your left side, with the foam roller on the floor and placed under the middle of your thigh. Support your torso with your left forearm on the floor.

Step 2 Bend your left leg and cross it in front of your right, so that your knee is pointed upward. Place your left foot flat on the floor.

Step 3 Pulling with your shoulder and pushing with your supporting leg, roll back and forth along the side of your thigh. Adjust the placement of your arm as you make your motion bigger.

Step 4 Repeat 15 times on each side.

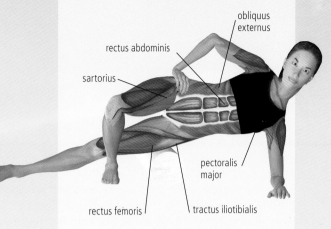

TARGET MUSCLES

obliquus externus

rectus abdominis

sartorius

pectoralis major

rectus femoris

tractus iliotibialis

ILIOTIBIAL BAND AND OBLIQUES

CORRECT ACTION
- Your shoulders remain relaxed throughout the exercise
- Your hands and forearms press firmly into the floor

AVOID
- Allowing your shoulders to lift toward your ears

Bridge with Leg Lift

The Bridge with Leg Lift is a great exercise for your glutes and hamstrings. Take care performing this movement, as there is the danger of the roller rolling out from under you—keep it in position using your abdominal and thigh muscles.

WARNING This exercise is not advisable if you have lower-back pain, a hamstring injury, or ankle pain.

Step 1 Lie on your back, with the roller under your shoulders. Your buttocks should be on the floor, with your knees bent, and feet flat on the floor.

Step 2 Press into the floor with your feet, and bridge up, lifting your hips toward the ceiling until they are parallel to the ground.

Step 3 Extend your left leg.

Step 4 Raise your left leg up to the height of your knees. Keeping your leg straight and the roller still, raise and lower your hips.

Step 5 Return to step one and repeat with the right leg.

Step 6 Repeat 15 times on each leg.

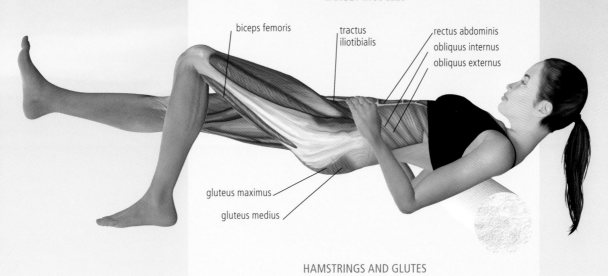

TARGET MUSCLES

biceps femoris

tractus iliotibialis

rectus abdominis

obliquus internus

obliquus externus

gluteus maximus

gluteus medius

HAMSTRINGS AND GLUTES

CORRECT ACTION
- Your extended leg remains straight

AVOID
- Allowing your hips and lower back to drop during the movement
- Arching your back

3

Bridge with Leg Lift II

This advanced version of the Bridge with Leg Lift is designed to help improve pelvic stabilization, strengthen your gluteal muscles, and strengthen your hamstrings. Focus on keeping the foam roller as immobile as possible.

WARNING This exercise is not advisable if you have lower-back pain, a hamstring injury, or ankle pain.

Step 1 Lie on your back, with the roller under your feet.

Step 2 Without moving the roller or arching your back, bridge up, and lift your hips into the air.

Step 3 Keeping your muscles firm, raise your right leg up to the height of your knees, and straighten your raised leg.

Step 4 Try to keep the roller from moving, and raise and lower your hips while keeping your outstretched leg raised. Repeat 15 times.

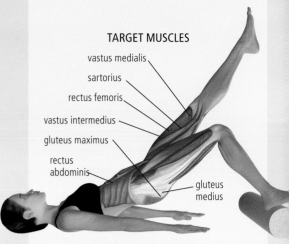

TARGET MUSCLES

vastus medialis
sartorius
rectus femoris
vastus intermedius
gluteus maximus
rectus abdominis
gluteus medius

PELVIS AND GLUTES

CORRECT ACTION
- Your shoulders and neck remain relaxed throughout the exercise
- Your extended leg remains straight

AVOID
- Allowing your shoulders to lift toward your ears
- Allowing your hips and lower back to drop during the movement
- Arching your back

Hamstring Pull-In

The Hamstring Pull-In is far more challenging than it looks at first glance. The difficulty lies in controlling the range of motion of the foam roller. That said, it provides a great workout for your hamstrings and glutes, increasing strength and endurance in both. It also helps to strengthen your pelvic stabilizers.

Step 1 Lie supine on the floor, your knees bent and the roller under your feet.

Step 2 Bridge up, lifting your hips so that they align with the shoulders in a neutral position.

Step 3 Squeeze your buttocks, and pull your calves in and out as you roll the roller under your feet.

Step 4 Repeat 15 times for two sets.

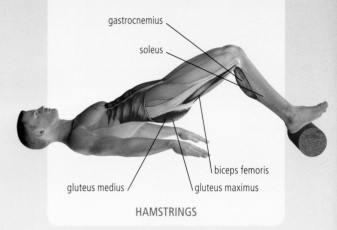

TARGET MUSCLES

gastrocnemius

soleus

biceps femoris

gluteus medius

gluteus maximus

HAMSTRINGS

CORRECT ACTION
- Your shoulders remain relaxed throughout the exercise
- Your body forms a straight line from shoulders to knees

AVOID
- Allowing your hips and lower back to drop as the movement is performed
- Arching your back

Straight-Leg Bicycle

The Straight-Leg Bicycle improves pelvic stabilization, and is a great abdominal-strengthening routine. It also works your thigh muscles. Try to keep your shoulders as flat to the roller as you can.

WARNING This exercise is not advisable if you have lower-back pain or neck pain.

Step 1 Lie on your back with the roller placed lengthwise under your spine, your buttocks and shoulders resting on the roller. Place your forearms on the floor on either side of the roller to balance yourself.

Step 2 Draw your knees up to a tabletop position, forming a 90-degree angle between your hips, thighs, and calves.

Step 3 Keeping your back flat, lift your head, neck, and shoulders off the roller. Straighten your right leg and pull your left knee in toward your chest, keeping your head, neck, and shoulders lifted.

Step 4 Switch legs while maintaining your balance, imitating the pedaling of a bicycle. Repeat 15 times on each leg.

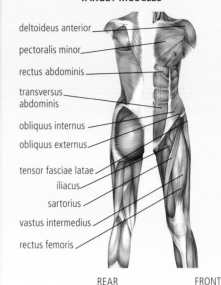

TARGET MUSCLES

deltoideus anterior
pectoralis minor
rectus abdominis
transversus abdominis
obliquus internus
obliquus externus
tensor fasciae latae
iliacus
sartorius
vastus intermedius
rectus femoris

REAR   FRONT

ABDOMINALS AND PELVIS

CORRECT ACTION
• Your neck remains relaxed throughout the exercise
• Fully extend your leg during the downward phase of the "pedaling" movement

AVOID
• Allowing your shoulders to lift toward your ears
• Lifting your hips and lower back during the movement

Dead Bug

The Dead Bug doesn't sound as though it should be especially challenging, but it certainly is! Be sure to do this on a padded mat, as the chances of rolling off are pretty high. It's worth persevering, though, as it's a great core-stabilizing workout.

WARNING This exercise is not advisable if you have lower-back pain or neck pain.

Step 1 Lie on your back with the roller placed lengthwise under your spine, your buttocks and shoulders resting on the roller. Place your hands and forearms flat on the floor for stabilization. Draw your knees up so that your legs form a tabletop position.

Step 2 Lift your head, neck, and shoulders.

Step 3 Press the palms of your hands onto your knees, creating your own resistance as you try to balance. Flex your toes and keep your elbows pulled in to your sides. Hold for 10 seconds. Repeat 10 times.

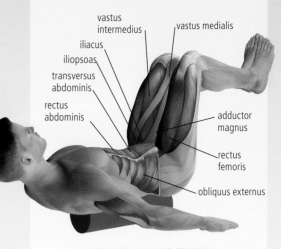

TARGET MUSCLES

vastus intermedius
vastus medialis
iliacus
iliopsoas
transversus abdominis
rectus abdominis
adductor magnus
rectus femoris
obliquus externus

ABDOMINALS AND THIGHS

CORRECT ACTION
- Your hips, thighs, and calves form a 90-degree angle
- Your neck remains relaxed throughout the exercise
- Your shoulders and buttocks remain flat on the roller throughout the exercise

AVOID
- Allowing your shoulders to lift toward your ears
- Lifting your hips or lower back during the movement
- Falling off the roller!

Workouts

The following thematic workouts take into account the differing goals and parameters one reading this book might have. Ranging in scope and intensity, they are thorough and challenging, and are great examples of how to put it all together in terms of chasing and achieving one's fitness goals. Be safe, take your time, and above all, have fun.

Beginner Workout

Suitable for all levels, especially those new to core training.

1 Crunch, p. 56

2 Alternating Crunch, p. 57

3 Russian Twist, p. 102

4 Leg Raises, p. 74

5 Quadruped Lateral Lift, p. 63

6 Hip Crossover, p. 33

7 Oblique Roll-Down, p. 62

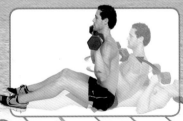

8 Dumbbell Sit-Up, p. 111

9 Body Saw, p. 98

Rotational Workout

This workout is designed to improve and strengthen one's rotational performance.

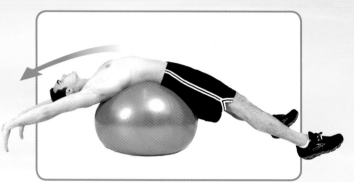

① Swiss Ball Abdominal Stretch, p. 19

② Russian Twist, p. 102

⑤ Alternating Sit-Up, p. 55

⑥ Bosu Ball Leg Scissors, p. 131

⑧ Diagonal Crunch, p. 140

⑨ Hip Crossover, p. 33

3 Seated Barbell Twist, p. 114

4 Side-Bend Plank, p. 82

7 Quadruped Knee Pull-In, p. 136

10 Standing Plate Twist, p. 115

Erector Workout

This workout is designed to strengthen the musculature of the core, with particular emphasis on the lower back.

1 Swiss Ball Pike, p. 26

2 Lemon Squeezer, p. 60

8 Big Circles with Medicine Ball, p. 38

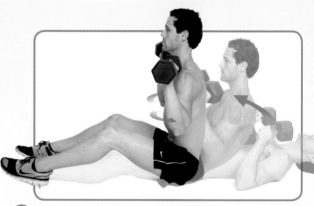

5 Dumbbell Sit-Up, p. 111

9 Turkish Get-Up, p. 108